S0-BYI-963

DIARY
OF A
HEDGEHOG

DIARY
OF A
HEDGEHOG

Biggs' Final Words on the Markets

BARTON BIGGS

WILEY

John Wiley & Sons, Inc.

Cover Background Image: © Ursula Alter/iStockphoto
Cover Illustration (hedgehog): © Igor Djorovic/iStockphoto
Cover design: Michael Freeland

Copyright © 2012 by Barton Biggs. All rights reserved.

Published by John Wiley & Sons, Inc., Hoboken, New Jersey.

Published simultaneously in Canada.

No part of this publication may be reproduced, stored in a retrieval system, or transmitted in any
form or by any means, electronic, mechanical, photocopying, recording, scanning, or otherwise,
except as permitted under Section 107 or 108 of the 1976 United States Copyright Act, without
either the prior written permission of the Publisher, or authorization through payment of the
appropriate per-copy fee to the Copyright Clearance Center, Inc., 222 Rosewood Drive, Danvers,
MA 01923, (978) 750-8400, fax (978) 646-8600, or on the Web at www.copyright.com. Requests
to the Publisher for permission should be addressed to the Permissions Department, John Wiley &
Sons, Inc., 111 River Street, Hoboken, NJ 07030, (201) 748-6011, fax (201) 748-6008, or online at
http://www.wiley.com/go/permissions.

Limit of Liability/Disclaimer of Warranty: While the publisher and author have used their best
efforts in preparing this book, they make no representations or warranties with respect to the
accuracy or completeness of the contents of this book and specifically disclaim any implied warranties of merchantability or fitness for a particular purpose. No warranty may be created or
extended by sales representatives or written sales materials. The advice and strategies contained
herein may not be suitable for your situation. You should consult with a professional where appropriate. Neither the publisher nor author shall be liable for any loss of profit or any other commercial damages, including but not limited to special, incidental, consequential, or other damages.

For general information on our other products and services or for technical support, please contact
our Customer Care Department within the United States at (800) 762-2974, outside the United
States at (317) 572-3993 or fax (317) 572-4002.

Wiley publishes in a variety of print and electronic formats and by print-on-demand. Some
material included with standard print versions of this book may not be included in e-books or in
print-on-demand. If this book refers to media such as a CD or DVD that is not included in the
version you purchased, you may download this material at http://booksupport.wiley.com. For
more information about Wiley products, visit www.wiley.com.

Library of Congress Cataloging-in-Publication Data:

Biggs, Barton, 1932-2012
   Diary of a hedgehog : Biggs' final words on the markets / Barton Biggs.
      p.   cm.
      ISBN 978-1-118-29999-9 (cloth) — 978-1-118-43176-4 (ebk) — 978-1-118-43178-8 (ebk)
      — 978-1-118-43160-3 (ebk) 1. Hedge funds. I. Title.
   HG4530.B5153   2012
   332.64'524—dc23
                                                                        2012033913

Printed in the United States of America
10 9 8 7 6 5 4 3 2 1

"He jests at scars who never felt a wound."
—*Shakespeare,* Romeo and Juliet *(Romeo at II, ii)*

"If anyone really knew they wouldn't tell you."
—*Anonymous*

A Personal Message to Readers

*T*hree days after the last entry in this diary, I spoke to my father on the phone and he told me he felt very ill. I was surprised, because he rarely admitted to feeling sick, but my concerns eased when he said he'd been to see his doctor, and had been given some medication for the flu. "This is really some flu, though," he told me, "I feel terrible."

A day and a half later, his condition had deteriorated to the point that he had to be rushed to the emergency room. Tests showed that rather than a flu, his symptoms were the result of a virulent staph infection that had probably entered his bloodstream through a minor cut or scratch.

There were periods of optimism over the next several weeks as he fought the infection with typical defiance and stoicism. But the illness, as well as some of the so-called cures, took a heavy toll on several of his vital organs, and it eventually became clear (to him before the rest of us) that this was a battle he wasn't going to win. He spent his last days at home, surrounded by close friends and his children, grandchildren, and extended family. On a pleasant Saturday evening, seven weeks to the day after our phone conversation, he died in his bedroom.

As the following pages make clear, my father believed that a great investor had to always be learning. He was a student of history and literature, and when discussing investing, it wasn't unusual for him to cite Frost or Yeats, or to draw on the lessons of a great battle from a historical war. Concepts from philosophy and psychology were as important to him as charts and statistics. He frequently likened investing to combat, and talked about investment survival in terms usually reserved for life and death issues. No doubt, much of his success as an investor can be attributed to his ability to apply the broader themes of life to his work.

Over these last months, however, I have learned that this relationship worked both ways; not only did knowledge and understanding of
the major themes of life help him to face investment challenges, but
experience with the great themes of investing helped him to face life's
challenges. I'm struck by the parallels between how my father faced the
difficulties of recent years as an investor, and how he faced the difficulties
of his final weeks of life. In both, he was a realist, able to assess a situation
with matter-of-fact reasoning and clarity. And while ever an optimist at
his core, in investing and in life, when it was time to face an unpleasant
reality, he did so with courage and conviction.

I confess that prior to this summer, I had wondered if my father was,
in some sense, terrified by death. He went to great lengths to stay young
for his years, keeping himself in excellent physical shape, and pursu-
ing activities like mountain climbing, tennis, and even touch football
long after most people his age had moved on to less rigorous pursuits.
Professionally, he had no interest in retirement, and intellectually, he
maintained a fresh point of view on modern culture and world events
when many of his contemporaries had slipped into the narrow, stale
thinking that is sometimes a symptom of age. So, while loving these
things about my father, I also wondered how he would react when he
had to face his own mortality.

He answered these questions for me as I spent time with him during
his final days. As death became inevitable, he seemed serene, accepting,
and perhaps even a bit eager to find out what was coming next. I sensed
calmness, clarity, and a gentleness towards those around him. I detected
no fear. After reading this book, I understand that it was his experience with facing questions of investment survival, those "life and death"
investment questions he stared down every day, that helped him to face
death with strength, courage, and dignity.

—Barton Biggs, Jr.

In Memoriam

Barton Biggs
November 26, 1932 – July 14, 2012

We at John Wiley & Sons are privileged to have published several books by Barton Biggs. Barton was an accomplished writer and a meticulous wordsmith. His first book, *Hedgehogging*, was a brilliant behind-the-scenes look at the players and the workings of Wall Street. For his next book, *Wealth, War & Wisdom*, Barton moved away from a discussion of the current markets to examine the intersection of financial crisis and the turning points of World War II.

We are especially pleased to publish *Diary of a Hedgehog*, which Barton completed shortly before his untimely passing. His observations on Wall Street were always illuminating, and this book is a collection of his investment commentary.

He reviewed the columns and provided introductory material before his death. The pages were then reviewed by his son, Barton Biggs.

Here are the books written by Barton Biggs.

Hedghogging
Wealth, War & Wisdom
A Hedgefund Tale of Reach & Grasp: or What's Heaven For?
Diary of Hedgehog: Biggs' Final Word on the Markets.

Contents

2012

Acknowledgments

The publisher, John Wiley & Sons, and I wish to thank Bank Itaú BBA for its generosity in letting us use the material I wrote for them in this book.

Introduction

*M*acro investing as I try to practice it is simple but never easy. It's not just about wrestling with the global environment and getting your asset allocation positioned. Good information, thoughtful analysis, quick but not impulsive reactions, and knowledge of the historic interaction among companies, sectors, countries, and asset classes under similar circumstances in the past are all important ingredients in getting the legendary "it," that we all strive so desperately for, right. A worldview is essential, but you don't have to be Henry Kissinger gazing out the window to the far horizons and thinking deep, world-shaking strategic thoughts.

Moreover, there are no relationships or equations that always work. Quantitatively based solutions and asset allocation equations invariably fail as they are designed to capture what would have worked in the previous cycle, whereas the next one remains a riddle wrapped in an enigma. The successful macro investor must be some magical mixture of an acute analyst, an investment scholar, a listener, a historian, and a riverboat gambler, and be a voracious reader. Reading is crucial. Charlie Munger, a great investor and a very sagacious old guy, said it best:

> I have said that in my whole life, I have known no wise person, over a broad subject matter who didn't read all the time—none, zero. Now I know all kinds of shrewd people who by staying within a narrow area do very well without reading. But investment is a broad area. So if you think you're going to be good at it and not read all the time you have a different idea than I do.

But the investment process is only half the battle. The other weighty component is struggling with yourself and immunizing yourself from the psychological effects of the swings of markets, career risk, the pressure of benchmarks, competition, and the loneliness of the long distance runner. We are all vulnerable in varying proportions to the debilitating and destructive consequences of these malignancies and there are no easy answers. Age and experience to a certain extent temper them but we are what we are. I've come to believe a personal investment diary is a step in the right direction in coping with these pressures, getting to know yourself, and improving your investment behavior.

Such a diary has to be written *in the heat of the moment, in the fire and agony of the time*, not retroactively or retrospectively. Its value comes from reading your thoughts and emotions later in the context of events and seeing where you were right and wrong. My writings for Itaú and my letters to investors are my investment diary of these crisis years that seem to drag on so interminably. As I scan through them, it's appalling and frightening how often I was influenced, swept away by the ebb and flow of the battle (and it is a battle—the battle for investment survival), and made bad decisions.

Mid-2010

FDR's Fiscal Policy Redux

After a very strong 2009, markets rallied briskly through most of April and a whiff of "maybe we are truly out of the woods" exhilaration swept through the still traumatized crowd, most of whom were still licking their wounds. We gained almost 6% in March, then abruptly a painful correction began at the beginning of May. Once again the chorus of "sell in May and go away" was heard.

We begin the diary in the first days of July 2010 with the S&P 500 down and the fund off 6.6% for the year to date. Not a happy time. As you will see, I was too cautious and as a result missed the first somewhat timid leg of the move higher that was developing. As usual, there were compelling arguments from both the bulls and the bears, but as markets fell, for uncertain souls like me the negative case became more compelling. Fortunately, long positions in U.S. energy stocks and in Asia kept me going. The gains of July were mostly retraced in August. The moral of the story is that you were probably better off to keep your powder dry until the fog of war lifted and then load up in late August, early September.

■ ■ ■

July 8, 2010

Equity markets and the high-frequency economic data around the world are weakening. Over the last couple of weeks, employment numbers, production indices, house price measures, and funding market stresses have been uniformly disappointing—and disconcerting. The S&P 500 sets the tone for the world, and in the last few days it has stumbled through the February and June correction bottoms reaching a new low for the year, and Treasury bond yields in both America and Germany are setting new lows. What's more worrisome is that it is beginning to appear that the so-called Authorities are on the verge of

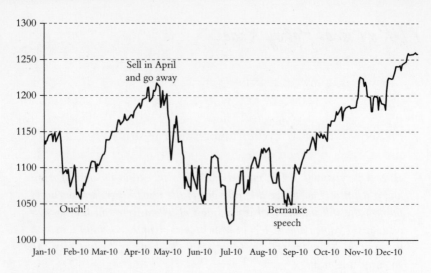

Keep Your Powder Dry

Data source: Bloomberg

making a serious policy error comparable to what occurred in the 1930s by prematurely tightening fiscal policy.

Until the last week or so the received wisdom was that the global economy after its powerful recovery was entering a "soft patch" for several quarters during which growth would continue but at a slower pace. It was generally conceded that the stimulus programs were beginning to run off and that the recovery was healthy but not yet self-sustaining. In other words, that the patient was still a little fragile. The European sovereign debt crisis and funding issues in the banking system also were creating some uneasiness. Meanwhile, in the U.S., consumer confidence was falling faster than expected and measures of economic growth such as retail activity, the PMIs and ISMs were clearly showing that the pace of growth, the so-called second derivative, almost everywhere was slowing. More ominously the ECRI leading indicator (which, incidentally, has had an excellent forecasting record) has collapsed to a 45-week low in the most precipitous slide in fifty years. Investors were beginning to get nervous although the businessmen we talked with in the U.S., Asia, and Europe were telling us of strong order flows and activity.

On the other hand, at this stage of a recovery cycle after a full-fledged financial panic, doubt and worry about the vibrancy of the economy are normal. The bears come out of the woodwork. Alan Greenspan made this very point last week in an interview on television. ISI points out that in September 1992 *Time* magazine, at a similar cyclical moment, wrote:

> The US economy remains almost comatose. The slump already ranks as the longest period of sustained weakness since the Depression. The economy is staggering under many structural burdens, as opposed to familiar "cyclical" problems. The structural faults represent once-in-a-lifetime dislocations that will take years to work out. Among them: the job drought, the debt hangover, the banking collapse, the real estate depression, the health-care cost explosion, and the runaway federal deficit.

This paragraph sounds like what the doomsayer economists whose last names begin with R on CNBC are saying today. The great economist Joseph Schumpeter liked to say: "Pessimistic visions about almost anything always strike the public as more erudite than optimistic ones." It turned out that the economy was in a temporary soft spot in the fall of 1992 and stocks were about to soar. In fact, one of the greatest bull markets in history was about to begin.

However, the new development in the current equation is the tightening bias of the Authorities and the extreme rhetoric and power of the austerity brigade. Just this past weekend the chairman of the European Central Bank (ECB), a moderate man, added his voice to the chorus. Although most of the savants are maintaining that additional fiscal juice is needed to prevent the present global "soft patch" from becoming a "double dip," the high priests of the temple who want us to be punished NOW for our sins with immediate pain and suffering are calling for no more stimulus.

As it has turned out, President Obama was the only leader at the G–20 meetings calling for more stimuli to sustain what he labeled as a "still developing recovery." Ironically, the president's own country is not listening. The Congress last week failed to extend unemployment insurance and is considering other measures to restrain spending. With the mid-term elections only months away and visions of Tea Parties dancing in their heads, partisan politics are affecting the willingness of many incumbent politicians to approve new spending programs. As it stands now, the U.S. will withdraw from both structural and cyclical forces about 4.5% of fiscal impetus from real GDP over the next five quarters as spending legislation and tax cuts expire.

At the same time, the other major economic powers are imposing fiscal austerity of one type or another to shrink budget deficits. To wit: the new U.K. government has presented a stringent emergency budget that adds to the tightening already in place another minus 4.3% of GDP; the new Japanese prime minister says he is going to restrain JGB issuance and raise taxes; and European fiscal policy is frantically moving towards the most aggressive tightening in more than four decades. The most extreme examples are Spain's, where fiscal impetus is targeted at minus 5.4%, Portugal minus 6.9%, and Greece minus 6.8%, with Germany, France, and Italy in the minus 2% area. However, bear in mind that the recovery from the recession in Europe (with the possible exception of Germany) is barely perceptible. Emerging Asia where the economic resurgence is by far the most firmly based also is justifiably tightening, and a few Asian central banks are actually hiking interest rates. On the other hand, China, the third largest economy in the world and one of the principal growth engines, seems to be attempting to reduce real GDP growth from its current 10–11% to 7–9% over the next four quarters.

Thus the worrywarts like me are afraid that the U.S. and the world are going to repeat the error that Franklin D. Roosevelt (FDR) made in the late 1930s. FDR, assailed by conservatives for his boondoggles and public spending programs and believing that the Great Depression was over, in early 1937 imposed tax increases and drastic spending cuts that took about 5% out of GDP—or about the same amount as we are doing now. Then industrial production plummeted, the economy aborted into another recession, and the stock market, which had tripled from its 1932 low, plummeted 50% and gave back over half of its gains in 15 months. Back then the German economy was the strongest major in the world and Europe in general was increasing defense spending as World War II loomed, so its fiscal policy was expansionary—not concretionary as it is today. However, back then there were no billion-population dynamos with high growth rates and potential like Indonesia and the BRICs (Brazil, Russia, India, and China) are today.

After a financial panic, severe recession, and a secular bear market such as we have experienced followed by an economic recovery and major stock market rally that retraces about half of the ground lost, it makes a lot of difference what then happens to the economy. At about the stage of the revival that we are in, it is normal for business activity and the stock market to become choppy as investors and businessmen are still licking their wounds. If after its big revival the economy transitions into nothing more serious than a soft patch of slower growth (say 2% to 3% real GDP for two to three quarters), investors worry but stocks usually pull back only 10% to 15% before surging again. However, if the economy suffers a "double dip" (two to four quarters of real GDP growth of only around 1.5% with no improvement in employment), then stocks can plunge 25% to 30% as everyone becomes really frightened that the stall will turn into another recession. If, heaven forbid, another recession actually occurs, then the declines can be far more severe as happened in the late 1930s. The bears are speaking of a testing of the lows of the spring of 2009.

Complicating the assessment is whether the environment is inherently inflationary or deflationary. For the time being, deflation seems to be more of a threat than inflation. As Japan has demonstrated, deflation is a very insidious plague because low or declining nominal GDP emasculates consumer spending (don't buy now because it will cost less later) and corporate profits. If the U.S. and the world slip back into a long stall or another recession, some episodes of deflation are probable. However, Jim Cramer's rants on CNBC about "deflation now" in my opinion are far too dramatic.

So what do I think is going to happen? Frankly, I'm not sure because, as noted, I am very concerned that governments and politicians are making a serious policy error by tightening fiscal policy. A massive dose of austerity makes about as much sense as the 18th- and 19th-century practice of bloodletting from deathly ill patients. Eventually we must reduce the size of government deficits and overall debt, but we need a self-sustaining expansion of the U.S. and global economy to be firmly ensconced before we start raising taxes and drastically reducing government expenditures. By moving prematurely, the Authorities are playing with fire and the outcome could be disastrous. Since I am an optimist (most of the time), I think we will come to our senses on policy. The global economy is frail but regaining its health, although the mature developed countries could be in for a "new normal" of slower, trend-line growth. However the emerging markets are a new and very positive force for world growth and for multinational companies. The BRICs are gradually transitioning from being export-dependent, commodity producers to domestic, consumer

Quarterly GDP growth forecasts

	2009				2010				2011			
	Q1	Q2	Q3	Q4	Q1	Q2	Q3	Q4	Q1	Q2	Q3	Q4
U.S.	−6.4	−0.7	2.2	5.6	2.7	3.5	2.0	1.5	1.5	2.0	2.0	2.0
MEU	−9.5	−0.5	1.6	0.2	0.8	2.5	1.5	1.0	1.0	1.0	1.5	1.5
UK	−10.0	−2.7	−1.1	1.8	1.2	2.5	2.5	2.0	1.5	1.5	1.5	1.5
Japan	−15.8	6.9	0.4	4.6	5.0	3.0	1.5	0.5	0.5	1.0	1.5	1.5
China	7.2	14.1	10.8	10.8	13.1	8.0	9.5	7.0	7.0	8.5	8.5	8.5
Rest of Emerging Markets	−10.5	5.7	8.0	8.1	4.5	8.3	5.5	4.4	0.4	4.5	5.0	5.0
Rest of Developed	−7.0	2.2	1.9	6.3	5.7	3.3	2.5	2.0	2.0	2.5	2.5	2.5
Developed	−9.2	0.4	1.5	3.2	2.3	3.0	1.8	1.2	1.2	1.5	1.7	1.7
WORLD	−7.9	2.9	3.8	5.2	3.9	4.6	3.2	2.4	2.3	2.7	3.1	3.1

Source: Traxis Partners LP

demand–driven growth. That's good. The only consistently profitable extractive industry is dentistry.

The table on page 8 summarizes our most likely outlook. As you can see, it envisions a mild double dip.

For the time being, I am reducing my exposure to equities very substantially. I think a long-only equity account should have its maximum permissible cash position. What would make me change my mind? Several months of rising employment numbers, a firming of house prices in the U.S., real progress on stress testing of European banks and the unlocking of the banking system, or another significant injection of fiscal or monetary (quantitative easing by the Fed) stimulus in the U.S. Obviously a further decline in stock prices and signs of panic selling would also be helpful. At this point my sense is that the aggressive money is beginning to understand the negatives I have outlined above but is not yet positioned for it.

Unfortunately bonds are not an attractive alternative at this point unless you believe a recession with whiffs of deflation is likely. Bonds are already priced for a double dip. Treasuries and bonds are overbought and most other fixed-income markets such as high yield and emerging market debt are extended. High-grade corporate bonds are the least unattractive category.

As for stocks, large capitalization, high-quality American equities with global franchises and good dividend yields are a fine place to be for the long run. In particular, big capitalization technology, capital equipment, oil service, pharmaceuticals, consumer cyclicals, and probably the REITs are attractive. Most major names in these categories are demonstrably cheap on earnings, free cash flow, true book value, and yield. Our studies indicate that only twice in the last hundred years have they been as cheap relative to the rest of the market. There is no urgency to buy them now, but unless you are running a hedge fund I would not disturb long-term positions. If the economy stumbles they will get cheaper.

As the forecast table suggests, emerging markets are still the place to be, but bear in mind that the great global multinationals are major participants in the developing economies. Warren Buffett has said he prefers to get his emerging market exposure through companies like Coca-Cola, McDonalds, etc. I prefer mine through more direct participation.

Chinese equities have had a big and, in my view, an unjustified correction. After a recent visit kicking the dusty tires, I am quite confident China is artfully managing its exchange rate, the economy, and asset prices for sustained progress. My affection also extends to many other Asian emerging markets and the BRICs, particularly India. The longer term, trend-line growth for Europe and Japan may only be 1.5%, for the U.S. 2.5%, but 5% for the developing world. That's a big difference!

Staying Close to the Shore

The sad truth is you may be right where the market is going, but you can't possibly predict where it will go after that. I was uncertain in July 2010 so I was staying close to shore and treading water. Don't forget you can be 200% wrong when you switch; sometimes twiddling your thumbs is the least malignant activity.

■ ■ ■

July 19, 2010

In the last two weeks the global economic outlook has deteriorated, and equity markets after an initial rally in early July faltered at the end of last week. I remain uninspired. It is too soon to tell whether the world economy is transitioning into a "soft patch" or a more serious "double dip." For the time being, what happens in the global economy in the next three to six months will rule financial markets. I will need more high-frequency data before changing my basic position, which is now to be around 40–50% net long equities in a hedge fund account and to be holding 15–20% cash in a long-only, benchmark-judged equity account. Being long Treasuries, bonds, and high-grade corporates is the same as being short equities. High-yield, distressed, and emerging market debt are directly correlated with equities, as are the industrial commodities. I have no strong convictions on currencies. Remember what Keynes said when he was questioned about his uncertainty. "When the facts change, I change my mind. What would you do, sir?"

The most recent high-frequency data indicates that global growth, which essentially rolled over in late May and early June, is now declining. In most cases this is the second derivative change—in other words a decline in the rate of change. Global manufacturing, which surged 12% from its low, is now expanding 7–8% on its way to perhaps 5%.

This can be construed as a "soft patch"—a normal correction at this stage of the recovery cycle as production aligns with final demand. If the recovery is truly self-sustaining, this pause should be followed after a few quarters by stronger gains as employment increases and credit flows. History suggests that if this benign outcome is the case, with the S&P 500 having fallen 18% and other markets around the world down by roughly similar magnitudes, the decline is probably about over.

What bothers me is that the financial panic and global recession we experienced were substantially more extreme than any post–World War II cycle. Everyone either has read or is reading Reinhart and Rogoff's book *This Time Is Different* (Princeton University Press, 2009), which argues forcefully that what's different ain't good. At this point, both the banking system and confidence are still suffering from a severe hangover that paralyzes capital spending, hiring, and the animal spirits of the commercial beast. It also casts a pall over the stock market. Since so many subliminally believe that the stock market is the best forecaster of the economy, a negative feedback cycle comes into play.

European banks' balance sheets and capital accounts are not healed, and at the end of last week there were renewed signs of stress in the interbank lending markets. Consumer confidence in America is very fragile. In fact, the University of Michigan survey that was released last Friday showed one of the steepest declines on record. Something like half to two-thirds of the swings in U.S. retail spending are driven by the top 10% of income families. As I have mentioned previously, house prices and stocks in the vast majority are what affect these people's net worth. It appears that in June the decline in the stock market had quite an effect. Unfortunately house prices don't look that healthy either, but we will know more this week.

Meanwhile the very latest data indicate sharp declines in industrial production around the world. It appears the pace of China's IP not only slowed in June but actually declined. This is a big deal! China is the growth engine of the world currently accounting for almost half of world GDP growth. If it conks out, global growth is going to come in much lower than now expected. At a small lunch last week, two very rich, very well-connected Chinese industrialists painted a sobering picture of the near-term outlook for the Chinese economy. They maintain that the government does not presently have the monetary tools to stimulate the economy because real estate is the lever of the transmission mechanism, and land and property prices are falling. The world needs a vibrant

China, and it is possible GDP growth, which was 10.8% in the first quarter and around 7.2% in the second, could fall to 4–5% in the second half of the year. The Chinese stock market has underperformed so far this year and is grossly oversold. I have a big position, and I am concerned.

Another important engine of world growth is emerging Asia, which over the past year has been expanding at a 10% pace. Now all of a sudden two of the biggest economies, Korea and Taiwan, are drastically slowing towards what I hope will be a 5% pace. Don't be misled by the very strong numbers posted by Singapore. It's a tiny economy. Japan is still a basket case and is now having to endure another emasculated prime minister and a hung parliament. Disinflation is almost everywhere, with the exception of India. Last week the U.S. reported the lowest inflation in 50 years. Remember Gibson's Paradox.

When inflation falls below 2%, it is no longer good for equities; it is bad and price-to-earnings ratios fall. What all this says to me is that the odds have increased to 50-50 not for a two-quarter pause, where world real GDP falls to 2–3% in a "soft patch," but a longer "double dip," where GDP growth slows to 1.5% and there are whiffs of deflation. Equity markets could have another 10% on the downside if the latter is the case. The high-frequency data on PMIs, ISMs, employment, and house prices will tell the tale. If we actually fell into another recession with mild deflation, prices could decline considerably further. This is what happened in 1938 after FDR tightened prematurely in 1937.

What keeps me awake at nights is the worry that the governments and central banks of the world, instead of alleviating the risks of a double dip or a recession within a recession, are compounding them by making a "policy error." Of course I believe we eventually will have to deleverage, write off the bad debt, recapitalize the banks, et cetera, but the sensible way to do it is to spread the pain over five to ten years rather than concentrate it in two years or three years of a Great Depression and a massive dose of Hegelian Creative Destruction. The global economy is too fragile, the political system too distended, the disparities between rich and poor too extreme. Revolutions and Barbarians at the Gates. Look what happened in the 1930s and then the 1940s. The Tea Party movement may just be a precursor.

The mistake the Authorities are making is that they are tightening fiscal policy and withdrawing stimulus at a time when the recovery is not self-sustaining and in fact is weakening. They should be pumping steroids into the system, not withdrawing them. The analogy is with a patient who has suffered a life-threatening infection. His doctors gave him powerful antibiotics and steroids. He began to recover and move around, and now he is eating again. His doctors, confident he is ready to stop the drug regime before it has run its course, are lecturing that drugs are bad for you. Of course you don't want to get hooked on them, but on the other hand, you want to be fully recovered before you go cold turkey. Now the poor guy is flushed, is running a low fever again, and is in a weaker position to fight the infection.

On the other hand, to repeat, I can seldom remember such overwhelming bearishness by the great wise men, professors, and stock market soothsayers. My experience has been that it is almost always right to bet against them when the consensus is the largest and the loudest. The surveys show that the hedge fund, aggressive investor world, although nervous, does not seem to be positioned for a major decline. As I said at the beginning, I would stay close to shore.

Stay Long but Watch the Ticks

Investing, whether aggressively or long term, is about averaging into a stance, whether bullish or bearish. Getting the timing exactly right when loading up or cutting back is a rare pleasure. As you will read, I am somewhat timidly moving towards a more fully invested stance. At this time I was gradually developing the confidence to build a major position in U.S. technology and was benefitting from being short Brazil and U.K. real estate.

■ ■ ■

July 26, 2010

I have increased my net long in equities from 50% to 75%, a posture I consider moderately but not wildly bullish. What has made me change my mind? I'm not making any money but it seems as though the clouds are lifting.

What has altered is that the economic data over the last ten days have been better than the experts' expectations. The global economy is showing surprising resilience, and Europe, supposedly the sick man of the world, is actually accelerating. One swallow doesn't make a spring, and the situation is still precarious, with whiffs of deflation, but the case for a soft patch rather than a double dip has strengthened. That's what equity and credit markets are focused on, and to the extent it continues, stocks will move higher, government and high grade corporate bonds will sell off, and high-yield and emerging-market debt spreads will contract.

Investor sentiment about equities is still depressed, pessimism about the economic recovery and President Obama is elevated, valuations are reasonable, and there is a huge amount of cash—public, institutional, and hedge fund—on the sidelines earning nothing. In essence, for the next few months owning equities may be the least bad alternative in an uncertain world. As a benchmark, the S&P 500 could have a rally up towards the top of its trading range for the year; in other words, a move

15

of 10–15% is conceivable. That's worth playing for. After that, we have to wait and see the shape of the global economy. Nothing is inevitable.

Last Friday European consumer confidence, retail sales, and industrial production numbers, instead of deteriorating as was forecasted, actually strengthened and in some cases were downright strong. Admittedly much of the gain was concentrated in the German economy, which constitutes over 40% of Euroland. The stress test results for the European banks released late Friday were positive, even if the rigor of the exam was not as intense in its treatment of sovereign debt holdings as some would have liked. In addition, real GDP in the U.K. rose 4.5% in the second quarter.

In the U.S., the high-frequency numbers are looking better. My two keys—employment and existing single-family home prices—are gradually improving. ISI's weekly company surveys of retail, capital goods, truckers, and construction all rose for the first time in almost a month. Admittedly they are still below their April highs. Companies continue to report superb second-quarter earnings, and, in general, second-half guidance is for more of the same. Corporate balance sheets are financial fortresses.

In non-Japan Asia and China, growth is coming off the boil and is settling back towards the trend of 5–6% for the former and 7–8% for the latter, but after all, there is nothing shabby about that. Eastern Europe continues to recover, but Japan is faltering again. Similar to the U.S., global GDP is soft-patching.

Finally, stock markets around the world have improved. To some it is heresy, but the truth of the matter is that for America, stock market action has been an excellent forecaster of the path of the economy and is included in the best leading indexes. This is not surprising when you recall that markets are a discounting mechanism, and they are a highly visible barometer of confidence for both businessmen and consumers. When we met with corporate executives over the last few weeks, they were telling us: "Our business is good and orders for the second half look strong. Before we came to New York, we were feeling confident but now after listening to the bearish economists, Wall Street, and CNBC, we are doubtful." Also, in the U.S. equities represent almost half of the spending class's net worth.

None of this is to say that we are out of the deep woods. The global economy is fragile. I'm still worried that the governments and central banks are making a serious policy error by tightening prematurely. The risk of deflation remains high, and government deficits, debt, and spending are out of control. There are bubbles out there that are yet to be popped. The U.S. economy has experienced the strongest recovery in nearly 30 years, but the recession was deeper than any since the early 1930s. Thus job creation and the breadth of the recovery are still depressed, and it remains to be seen how the people in the developed economies will react to sticky, high unemployment and benefit deductions.

However, there is no use in our beating our breasts indefinitely. There could be an opportunity here. I still think non-Japan Asia is the growth cockpit of the world. The Chinese H share market (an index of the major Chinese companies that is heavily weighted towards the banks) and Hong Kong may be turning as China takes its foot off the brake. Korea and Taiwan have discounted a slowdown in economic growth from almost 10% to 5%, and markets such as Indonesia and Thailand (particularly the banks) look attractive. Emerging markets should be a major destination for long-term money, particularly Brazil, Russia, Poland, and Turkey.

In the U.S., as I have previously discussed, big-capitalization, high-quality stocks are unusual long-term investment values. This group ranges from the great consumer franchise names to capital goods and technology companies such as Caterpillar, United Technologies, and Cisco. I suggest reading Jeremy Grantham's latest letter on the Web (Jeremy Grantham Summer Essay). Grantham is an original and great thinker, and his long epistle is worth digesting and thinking about. He writes that there is a possibility of a run back towards the highs of 2000 and 2007, which could then be followed by the apocalypse. I have also added to my holdings of certain large-cap U.S. technology stocks (a new equipment cycle is beginning), pharmaceuticals, REITs, and oil service.

This Is No Time to Get Wobbly, George!

As the old saying goes, the trouble with the stock market is not that it is controlled by mathematical factors, or that it is controlled by non-mathematical factors, but that it is controlled by both. This is what I was writing in mid-August.

■ ■ ■

August 16, 2010

After an episode of generally uplifting economic reports, the most recent round of high-frequency data from the U.S. have been soft. In addition, equity investors have been disconcerted and high-grade bond buyers emboldened by the Fed's token quantitative easing (which shows the Fed is worried), new problems in the Irish banking system, and some widening of credit spreads. Industrial commodities are selling off, and even the wise Doctor Copper is looking queasy. Not all was bleak, however, as Germany and Hong Kong reported real GDP growth for the second quarter at annual rates of 9% and 7.1%, respectively, and consumer confidence and fiscal revenues rose in China. Nevertheless, the consensus estimate of real GDP growth for America has been downgraded to 2% for the next four quarters. It is evident that the economies of the world and the U.S. are in a soft patch, and that pricing power is slowly evaporating, which means that inflation is drifting towards zero.

I would argue that with ten-year U.S. Treasury bonds at 3.5%, the German Treasury bonds (known as Bunds) yielding even less, and high-grade stocks at ten to twelve times earnings and seven or eight times free cash flow, the soft patch has been discounted. The issue that will drive markets is what happens next. Is the world headed for the dread double dip, with more than whiffs of deflation? A number of serious and vocal economists believe so. Nouriel Roubini said last week that the "sick man is Europe" and "something more than leaves will fall in Europe this

18

autumn . . . as governments crumble." Two other heroes of the bears, Reinhart and Rogoff, published a scholarly book entitled *This Time Is Different*, ostensibly proving that when gross government debt exceeds 90% of GDP (where the U.S. will be by year-end), not only does this level of debt mean slower long-term growth but fiscal stimulus loses its potency.

The truth is that no one knows. Everyone is just guessing. Last Thursday, the *Wall Street Journal* headlined that "Economists are Getting Pessimistic about the Strength of the US Recovery." No kidding! The gloom and doom are everywhere, with the so-called mouth-bet consensus becoming 1.5% real GDP growth, whiffs of deflation, and nominal GDP of zero to 2%. If that happens, such low nominal GDP numbers will wreak havoc with corporate profits! The more newly born bears often cite an analysis by Goldman Sachs of the likely profile of fiscal stimulus withdrawal in the U.S. over the next four quarters, still assuming tax cuts extended below $250,000, as follows:

Minus 0.75% in current quarter
Minus 1.25% in fourth quarter
Minus 1.50% in first quarter 2011
Minus 1.75% in second quarter 2011

Assuming that these numbers are right, and our work suggests they probably are, there will be a substantial drag on GDP in the next 12 months. For America, where consumer spending is 70% of GDP, employment and confidence are the key variables as he and she gradually deleverage. The positives are that the savings rate has now climbed back up to over 6%, employment and hours worked are gradually improving, house prices and consumer confidence seem to be stabilizing, and, with the corporate sector bulging with cash, capital spending should be on the rise. A double dip would require businesses again to cut back on inventories, capital spending, and employment, which seems very unlikely since they just did that and have so much liquidity. In addition, oil prices are soggy. There is always the possibility that the Obama administration will do something to stimulate the economy like partial mortgage forgiveness, but there are big negatives to drama.

The rest of the world also seems to be doing a little better. Even Greece is making progress. It's not yet time to strike our colors on the economy. The economic data are episodic and patchy. For two weeks they're bad; then they could swing to be positive again. Everyone is confused and uncertain. Ed Hyman, the economist most highly respected by institutional investors, told me Friday that he didn't know what to make of things. On the other hand, ISI and Ed cut their forecast for the second time in three weeks, to 2%, on Friday.

However, bear in mind that the public, institutional investors, and hedge funds have near record amounts of cash. They aren't earning anything on it! No one has made any money this year. Clients are getting restless. We hedge fund folks can't afford to miss the next move.

How do I feel? Uncertain, uneasy, whipsawed, buffeted. However, the one thing I do know is that a diversified list of high-quality global multinationals is very cheap on earnings and free cash flow, and provides a yield about 50 basis points higher than the 10-year Treasury bond. Incredible! Stocks represent ownership of real earning assets and franchises all over the world. Bonds are pieces of paper and governments are printing more paper. This group of stocks sells at a price/earnings ratio of around 10.5 times five-year earnings while the median PE over the last half century has been about 18 times. Previous bear market bottoms in 1990 and 2002 were made at 15 times. Even including the huge 2009 rally, Treasury bills have beaten stocks by 360 bps a year over the last decade. High-grade bonds are somewhere in a bubble of epic proportions. Of course, the question is where.

In any case, I'm still 75% net long equities. I'm tempted but afraid to short bonds. In the summer of 1990, the day after Iraq invaded Kuwait, President George H.W. Bush met with Prime Minister Margaret Thatcher in Aspen, Colorado, where they were attending the Aspen Institute conference. Financial markets around the world were in turmoil. The president was worried and uncertain what their response should be. Thatcher was, as always, resolute, defiant, and confident about what they should do. "This is no time to get wobbly, George," she told him. On several occasions when we were both on Julian Robertson's Tiger board I experienced directly the force of the Baroness's personality and convictions. Her words were always formidable and compelling. George Bush's wobbles ceased. I'm trying to keep from letting the short-term momentum swings in the data and the stock market from making me wobbly.

Make No Mistake: More QE Is Big Stuff

August 30, 2010

S tock markets continue to struggle, looking deathly ill one day and then rallying the next. Volatility and synchronicity across markets and sectors are extreme. It's investment anarchy, and gloom-and-doom about the future pervades as the chattering classes compete for the darkest sackcloth and ashes. Meanwhile high-grade bonds reach for the sky.

Everyone now knows the U.S. and global economies are in a soft patch; the issue is whether we are going into the dread double dip. Double dip means at least a couple of quarters of negative real GDP growth with whiffs of deflation and, of course, major downward revisions of corporate earnings and financial accidents. With the Authorities having expended both their fiscal and monetary ammunition, the sophisticates predict political paralysis, disillusionment, and Japanese-style slump-deflation. The more pessimistic envision frightening social consequences and a collapse of the already fragile fabric of confidence in the Western democracies. China, India, and the developing economies will be staggered, they say, and their equity markets are over-valued, so they are not safe havens. In the short run, the bears' asset stocks are oblivious to the impending downturn, the loss of corporate pricing power, and the bursting of the China growth bubble. At the same time technicals are deteriorating, U.S. dollar strength will be a headwind for Asian equities, and seasonality is poor.

William Butler Yeats's famous poem "The Second Coming" echoes eerily back across the years, although as yet there is no blood-dimmed tide, but certainly these days the best lack all conviction. At a recent dinner that I attended hosted by Ed Hyman with 12 eminent successful hedge fund managers, the majority argued we were in a secular (not cyclical) bear market and grimly muttered about a retest of the 2009 lows and years of malaise. They were the ones full of passionate intensity. Treasury bonds, credit default swaps, issuer-specific fixed-income trades, and gold were their vehicles. We relative bulls were mute and tongue-tied.

> Turning and turning in the widening gyre
> The falcon cannot hear the falconer;
> Things fall apart; the centre cannot hold;
> Mere anarchy is loosed upon the world,
> The blood-dimmed tide is loosed, and everywhere
> The ceremony of innocence is drowned;
> The best lack all conviction, while the worst
> Are full of passionate intensity.

As for me, I'm still hanging in there, about 75% net long equities, sporting a 4% loss for the year. The most recent high-frequency releases in the U.S. were depressing. Particularly disturbing were the data on the housing market. Although mortgage rates are at record lows, lenders have become obsessively conservative, and prospective buyers are paralyzed with fear. Joe Nocera, an astute but dark soul, had a devastating article in last Saturday's *New York Times* detailing the huge, shadow inventory of unsold homes, and the total freezing up of confidence and credit. The price of existing single-family homes and unemployment are the two key indicators of the animal spirits of the U.S. consumer.

Thus it is not surprising that the growth of both U.S. and global retail sales has slowed, and at the same time, the decline in the global services PMI indicates a slowing in services as well. The only bright spot is Germany, which reported a strong 3.9% annualized gain for second quarter GDP. Although more recent data such as consumer confidence surveys don't yet show signs of any deterioration, economists are warning that, as J.P. Morgan said, "It seems inevitable that the Euro-area economy will slow in the coming quarters."

So why am I still fairly fully invested? Focusing on the U.S. as the market and economy that still drives the world, don't forget that America is fundamentally a very robust system that is awash in liquidity and that has had ten very tough years. Don't bet against America and count the president out. As noted in my previous essay, the spending levels of both consumers and business are so low that they are unlikely to crater again. Both sectors are literally bulging with liquidity, and free cash flow as a percent of nominal GDP is at a 30-year high. Delinquencies on credit card debt are down big time, the major banks have reserve coverage of 1.4 times, and the latest Fed survey shows there is plenty of bank credit available, although the flow is still disappointing. Inventories have been drawn down again, the savings rate has snapped back, and capital spending never recovered. For the economy to fall into another recession, with the exception of housing, the excesses to cause it are simply not there. I think the odds of a true double dip are one in four.

The more sanguine case is that we are in the early stages of a powerful, cross-border M&A cycle, and as the Dell and HP contest shows, it's not just resources. M&A can catapult prices not just for the target but for similar firms. The public, institutions, pension funds, hedge funds, and private equity firms have immense amounts of cash on which they are earning virtually nothing and for which their clients are paying fees, in some cases fancy fees. Last week at the Fed's Jackson Hole conference the chairman of the Fed made it clear that if the data deteriorate further the Fed will do quantitative easing (QE).

Most of the attendees at the dinner I mentioned didn't think that QE would do much good and might actually be interpreted bearishly by markets. I think they're wrong. When the Bank of Japan (BOJ) finally did QE in 2002, the sickly Japanese economy stabilized and the Nikkei Index went from 8,000 to 18,000. When the BOJ pulled back from QE several years later, the Nikkei ran out of steam. As Hyman pointed out at the dinner, in March 2009 when the S&P was at its lows and all was gloom-and-doom, the Fed announced QE. His surveys at the time showed most people believed it wouldn't help either the economy or the stock market. Instead both stocks and the economy had powerful recoveries. QE, in addition to reviving the housing market, could also cause a rise in inflationary expectations that dramatically diverts fund flows from bonds to equities, and it could create renewed weakness in the dollar, which would be positive for U.S. earnings and exports. Chairman Bernanke's commitment to more QE if needed is very sweet music to equity investors' ears. I'm not sure if QE can single-handedly cure the anemic economy, but my guess is it won't take long for the stock market to figure out that it's bullish for equities. Say hello to the rally!

As for me, over half of my net long is in non-Japan Asia and other emerging economies that are still growing and have not had consumer spending and housing bubbles. Moreover, I do own high-quality big-capitalization inexpensive U.S. and European multinationals that have significant and expanding exposure to the developing markets and that have yields generally well in excess of the 10-year Treasury bond. However, I concede it is unrealistic, despite the gradual transition to domestic demand evolving across Asia, to expect that these export-intensive economies and their stock markets can weather a collapse in the West. I do own some 10-year U.S. Treasury bonds as a hedge against my long equity positions, but I have a very itchy finger. My intuition is that there are too many bears and too much liquidity. As they say, often wrong, always in doubt, but don't apologize for relying on your intuition if you've spent 40 years trying to develop it.

The Best and the Brightest Are Still Licking Their Wounds

After a financial panic, it's perfectly normal for the participants who are still alive to be shell-shocked. It's also usual that the public and investors in general do not sell and redeem at the bottom of the decline in prices. Then, however, as the equity market stalls, they begin to sell, and sell with considerable intensity. A year later and sometimes many years later, professional investors both young and old, unseasoned and experienced, are stunned by the impact and violence of the collision. Here I recount the state of my world in the fall of 2010.

■ ■ ■

September 10, 2010

Here we are three quarters of the way through the year and almost no one has made any money. The investment environment is still extremely tender. The grievous wounds of the savage bear market are still open and raw, and a lot of blood has been spilled and confidence lost. The public is redeeming traditional, long-only equity funds and feverishly buying bond funds. Pension and sovereign wealth funds are disillusioned with stocks and private equity. They grudgingly and painfully are conceding that their long-term return assumptions were too high, and that they can't meet their actuarial requirements. Fixed income (everything from high yield to Treasuries) is in vogue, and the giant pension and sovereign wealth funds are reducing their already low allocations to equities. PIMCO is hot, Bill Gross is the new Messiah, and his "New Normal" of years of mid-single-digit returns is the conventional wisdom. Heck, maybe they're right!

What about hedge funds, the stardust kissed golden child of the last decade? In late 2007, according to Hedge Fund Research, worldwide hedge fund assets reached US$1.9 trillion and there were around 10,000 funds. Today HFR estimates assets have declined to US$1.6 trillion and there are roughly 8,000 hedge funds. By 2007, the fastest growing segment of the hedge fund universe was the fund-of-funds business, which was compounding at a stunning 25% a year, and at the time accounted for 40% of hedge fund assets. HFR estimates there were 2,500 of them, up from 500 seven years earlier. Today their assets under management have declined at least 50%.

Hedge funds, like almost everyone else, had a savage bear market. For the year 2008, the hedge fund averages were off 20% to 25%, but with a mile-wide dispersion of individual results; and at the bottom, in March 2009, 30% drawdowns from the peaks of 2007 were common. Rumors of enormous liquidity problems circulated, the Madoff Ponzi scheme terrified everyone, hedge funds died right and left, and a number of large and famous funds raised "gates" while others reverted to "side pockets." A side pocket is when a fund moves an illiquid or loss-plagued investment out of its portfolio for performance reporting purposes and suspends withdrawals.

All this skullduggery enraged investors, and their stunning losses surprised and frightened them. They actually believed hedge funds would make money in a bear market because they had in 2000–2003. In addition, many of these investors had used funds of funds, which added another layer of fees and expenses. Even worse, some foolhardy souls had leveraged their holdings. In the last 18 months, feeling betrayed, wealthy individuals pulled out almost half of their money. The demise of both the fund-of-funds industry and hedge funds was forecast.

In contrast, the pension funds, endowments, and foundations that thought of hedge funds as another asset class in their portfolios were not so unhappy. Their traditional long-only managers were generally down 42–45%, in line with the indexes, and their emerging market managers lost more than 50% with a maximum drawdown at the March 2009 bottom of over 60%. Private equity, real estate, venture capital, and commodities were down at least as much—if they could be valued—and, to add insult to injury, were making capital calls. The so-called "Yale Model" was in disrepute. All things considered, hedge funds with losses of around 20% were the best of a disappointing lot.

Then after a ghastly January and February, along came the rally of 2009. The Dow Jones Industrial Average was up 21% and the S&P 500 16%. Hedge funds did OK, with the mean up 23%. According to Morgan Stanley, for the years 2008 and 2009 the hedge fund mean eked out a 6% gain, whereas the S&P 500 was down 20% and the UBS Commodity

Index lost 25%. The true returns from the less liquid asset classes like private equity, venture capital, and real estate are still being sorted out.

On the other hand, if you had been in the 10-year U.S. Treasury bond for the same two years, you would have had a total return of 16.2%, and even in high-yield, junk bonds you would have earned 13.6%. Fixed income clearly was the place to be. Is it still? I don't think so. The 10-year Treasury bonds and bunds at current yields are saying that the trend-line inflation rate in the U.S. and across northern Europe is going to be around zero. Seems highly unlikely to me. In my heart I think it's blowing a fantastic bubble to sell short, but previous painful experiences have taught me that I'm often early.

So what's happening now? Money is starting to flow back to hedge funds from big institutions around the world but it's very picky money. Start-ups that were in vogue during the glory years are dying on the vine and the existing medium-size funds are seeing only a trickle, and that's into a few hot asset categories such as emerging-market debt. Instead the big flows are to the giant hedge fund firms that have been relative winners; interestingly, the money is going mostly to one group, the least risky strategies.

Empirical Research Partners, the premier strategy research boutique, has assembled a data base of the monthly performance histories for the last decade of the majority of today's largest hedge funds. They then segmented the funds into high volatility and low volatility cohorts. The former tend to be aggressive macro investors willing to take big positions, mark time, and swing their net long around. The latter group run relatively low net long ratios and rely on grinding out alpha through stock selection with an extensive long and short portfolio. Over the course of the last decade, the high-volume group produced returns of +15% a year, but had a standard deviation of 17.5% and lost money in 34% of all the months. The stock market as a whole, both in the U.S. and Europe, had similar volatility but returns of 1.6% annually. The low-volume gang generated +11% per annum, but produced a standard deviation of only 5% and lost money in only 11% of the months. After the last three years, the returns of both groups are trending lower.

Now guess what? The low-volume, lower-return cohort of big funds ($5 billion or more) is getting most of the money. After a decade in which there was incredible volatility and two secular bear markets, the big institutions and sovereign wealth funds want more stability and less agony and ecstasy, and are willing to sacrifice a lot of performance in order to get it. Remember that it was the deity, Warren Buffett, who famously said that he would take a bumpy compounded 14% return over a smooth 9–10% every time, almost suggesting it would be irrational not to if you were a long-term investor.

Of course the other factor is that with all the gurus predicting an era of mid-single-digit returns in both stocks and bonds, fiduciaries with actuarial requirement of 7–8% are desperately looking for an asset class where they can get bond-like returns of that magnitude. It's an amazing switch that hedge funds are becoming bond substitutes, but that's what seems to be happening! Meanwhile small- and medium-sized hedge funds are dropping like flies, not so much because of performance but because their principals aren't making a living wage.

As for the start-ups, it's very tough to raise seed money, and in the new era of regulation and registration with the SEC, a fund has to have at least US$500 million of fee-paying assets to be viable. Already there are signs of fee pressure, and it is not inconceivable that 2 and 20 (2% fixed, 20% of profits) is going to shrink to 1 and 15. Brokers and third-party marketers are getting paid more, and the funds of funds are discounting their fees.

I don't believe that this new trend toward big, low-volume funds is going to work or last. This is self-serving because my fund is medium-sized, but the history is that most big funds in the long run become unglued for one reason or another, and once again it will be the up-and-coming, nimble newcomers who put up the big numbers in the future. The old adage that size is the enemy of performance is still true, and success and great riches have turned many a brilliant head. Hubris is as much a threat as Mr. Market. But I don't want to be dismissive. Stan Druckenmiller, who has run Duquesne (full disclosure: Stan is family) with spectacular success for many years, recently announced his retirement. Stan is closing Duquesne because he wants to do other things and because his fund had become unwieldy. Running other people's money wears on you, particularly if you like them. Also, many of the hedge fund elite genuinely want to do some good for the world with their fortunes. Nevertheless, an investor like Druckenmiller is irreplaceable and his clients will have to find someplace to go.

What are hedge funds thinking now? Generally speaking, we are licking our wounds and struggling with not having much to show for this year. For what it's worth, the ISI survey showed that during the last week U.S. hedge funds reduced their net long fairly sharply. The prime brokers report similar trends in Europe and Asia. Most hedgies currently lack conviction. Incidentally, that's a good sign, not an ill omen. The hedge fund net long has become an important contrary sentiment indicator.

Nobody Can See His Own Backswing

September 27, 2010

E quity markets are finishing a strong September, and the question on investment minds now is whether this rally is just one more false dawn within the uncertainties of the trading range or the precursor of a more sustained move. I'm inclined to the latter view. I like the disdain and jaundiced "sell the rally" advice that is being dispensed from prop traders, the media, and technicians who were not there. "Buy the dips and trim the rips" is still the conventional wisdom, which is healthy from a contrary point of view.

While the economic data continue to be mixed, in general it has a somewhat more positive bias. The high-frequency data suggest that odds of the U.S. careening into the dread "double dip" have diminished, although the current soggy "soft patch" persists. Stronger data last week included ISI company surveys, leading indicators, and capital goods shipments. On the other hand, I'm worried about the crucial index of the price of existing single-family homes, where 60% of the average American's wealth reposes. August sales and prices were soft.

The recent releases from China and (last week) Taiwan, as well as from some of the other large developing economies, suggest that a successful "soft landing" is underway. However, after having carried the ball for the last six months, Europe (even Germany) is suddenly looking a little sluggish. Japan, the third-largest economy in the world, continues to stumble along ineptly. Quantitative easing (QE) is still likely from the U.S., the U.K., and Japan.

Spreads in fixed-income markets continue to gradually tighten, although new worries about the Portugal, Ireland, Greece, and Spain (PIGS) seem to surface weekly. Retail and institutional investors continue to prefer bonds to stocks. My view is that government bond yields in the so-called "safe" countries around the world are ridiculously low.

For example, the yield on the 10-year benchmark Swiss issue is 1.35%. Government bonds historically have returned around 2% real, so investors must be expecting a decade of deflation or a very strong currency. The bias of politicians, central bankers, and people is always towards an inflationary—not deflationary—solution to their sins. However, from painful past experience I have learned that bubbles can get bigger and last longer than I can imagine, so I'm not yet up for shorting Treasury bonds.

My sense continues to be that in the U.S., while businessmen are seeing some improvement in both sales and orders, they have been unnerved by the gloomy "secular bear market" wailings from Wall Street and the famous bearish economists. A positive development for the economy would be a continuing, gradual rise in the stock market. Of course, gains in employment and a stabilization of the price of existing single-family homes are the crucial fundamental indicators, and both issues are still in doubt. More clarity on tax rates for next year and less confrontational rhetoric from the Obama administration would also be helpful, and both could happen. Corporate guidance and earnings forecasts are being revised down, but my hunch is that investors already know.

What's the magnitude of the advance I am sticking around for? Maybe 10% in the major averages. Since the beginning of September, equity fund flows have turned positive but have been concentrated in exchange-traded funds. Hedge funds, not the public or institutional investors, have propelled this rally so far, and according to the prime brokers, hedge funds are afflicted with low net longs and substantial short portfolios. There is a lot of potential fuel out there for higher prices if some of the clouds lift. Bear in mind that Mr. Market is both contrary and sadistic and thus loves to inflict the maximum amount of discomfort and pain on his worshippers. At least for now, the pain trade is up.

Fire and Ice

I have always loved Robert Frost's succinct and sensitive poetry, and "Fire and Ice" captures the dilemma of both human and economic experience. I may be stretching the analogy here, but perhaps not. An economic policy of Austrian austerity and the ensuing "Creative Destruction" would burn off the debris quickly, in searing flames in a couple of years of deflation, breadlines, and massive capital destruction. A mix of reform and monetary and fiscal stimulus should result in a new ice age of stagnation and no growth. Pick your poison. Japan since 1990 is an example of the latter alternative. Anyway, it's a wonderful poem, although not particularly cheery, and it rhymes in my soul.

■ ■ ■

October 11, 2010

Global equity markets, keying off the S&P 500, have climbed over the last six weeks, and another round of quantitative easing (QE) is expected shortly. It had better come or markets will feel betrayed. The high-frequency economic data from the U.S., Europe, and the developing countries indicate continuing slowing of the pace of the recovery but it has not been negative, and, to repeat, a fragile conviction is growing that the dread double dip is not developing. Meanwhile Treasury bond prices and fixed-income markets have gradually improved. However, with 10-year government yields less than 2.4%, bond buyers are implicitly forecasting further disinflation and even mild deflation. Thoughtful investors and serious commentators such as *The Economist* and the *Wall Street Journal* are still very uneasy about the longer-term outlook and repeatedly warn that there could be an apocalypse out there. Although I'm bullish short term for all the reasons I have previously cited, I'm plagued by their dark visions.

In the early 1930s, Robert Frost, an American poet and a New Hampshire mystic, who had, as he put it, "a lover's quarrel with the world" and who believed life was "a trial by existence," became deeply pessimistic about the future and wrote the following short verse, titled "Fire and Ice." I suspect (but of course don't know) that, for Frost, fire was the Nazi conflagration sweeping across Europe, and ice was the deflation that was ravaging the world.

> Some say the world will end in fire,
> Some say in ice,
> But from what I've tasted of desire
> I hold with those who favor fire.
> But if I had to perish twice,
> I think I know enough of hate
> To say that for destruction ice
> Is also great
> And would suffice.

This time, what will be the final outcome of the present Great Financial Crisis? Fire (inflation) or ice (deflation)? Or is terrorism the modern equivalent of ice? In the last few weeks, two very intelligent, thoughtful men, John Paulson and John Makin, have expressed extreme and radically different views of the direction the West is going. Both views are ominous, but each also presents tremendous investment opportunities. Depending on which is right, asset selection and therefore investment performance and wealth preservation over the next few years will be a life or death experience. Of course there is always the more hopeful possibility that the final outcome will be less extreme and more benign.

Neither Paulson nor Makin is a media babbler or crazed promoter attempting to attract attention and publicity. Makin is a visiting scholar at the American Enterprise Institute in Washington, D.C. He has been a consultant to the Treasury and the Congressional Budget Office, and is one of the most highly respected macroeconomists in the world. Paulson runs a huge hedge fund that had a brilliant record throughout the bear market, and was right for the right reasons. With exquisite timing, he made billions by going short subprime mortgages. Now some mealy-mouthed skeptics, perhaps with a touch of jealousy, argue he may be "a one-trick pony" but his record speaks for itself. Admittedly, Makin is not a professional investor the way Paulson is, but at the lunch with him that

I attended, it was clear that not only is he a very intense analyst and economic historian, he also is deeply involved with markets and is not just an academic. I take what both say very seriously. This is not posturing or some form of trivial pursuit.

Makin argues that financial crises from bursting bubbles are inherently deflationary "because they create a rise in the demand for cash that depresses aggregate demand at a time when substantial excess capacity exists." Today, because of this toxic combination, he says, the developed Western economies are caught in a deflationary cycle that is spiraling out of control. This current spiral is being intensified by the policy errors of the so-called Authorities—the politicians and central banks. The same thing happened in the 1930s and again in Japan in the 1990s.

Five to seven years ago when the bubble was growing, the huge flows of what Keynes once called "stupid money" resulted in the underpricing of risk, which, Makin points out, lowers the cost of capital and leads to the over-building of the capital stock and eventually to a large capacity gap. Households, stimulated by cheap, available credit, overspend; buy excessive numbers of cars, houses, and things; and reduce their savings rate. When the bubble finally bursts, wealth in the form of stocks and house prices is destroyed. As the economy falters, workers are laid off so they cut spending and increase savings. With an excess supply of capacity and goods, prices, rents, and wages begin to fall.

At the same time, there is a huge increase in the demand for cash. A crisis causes a sharp rise in uncertainty and banks become unwilling to lend and borrowers to borrow. As Makin puts it: "Excess capacity adds to the deflationary pressure induced by a sharp increase in the demand for money and the disintermediation that accompanies a financial crisis and its aftermath."

Thus even though the Fed frantically prints money, the money multiplier collapses and the money supply stagnates. This, he says, is why the "Doves," who argue that the sharp rise in the size of the Fed's balance sheet is inflationary, are wrong. However, a deflation and depression are not inevitable if only the Authorities would do the right thing. In a piece published last summer by AEI, he wrote succinctly what central banks, particularly the European Central Bank, should take note of:

Financial crises are usually deflationary. Pretending otherwise because of a policy of low interest rates and sharp increases in the monetary base after financial bubbles have burst constitutes a necessary, although not sufficient condition for a global depression. This would be especially true if China's response to the crisis was to create more excess capacity while refusing to allow its currency to appreciate. A persistent failure to respond to the dangers of further deflation, such as the premature removal of accommodative monetary policy by the ECB or a sharp fiscal contraction favored by the European Monetary Union, would sharply elevate the risk of global deflation and depression.

At this point in the post bubble transition to deflation, fiscal rectitude and monetary stringency is a dangerous combination, as appealing as they may be to the virtuous instincts of policymakers faced with a surfeit of sovereign debt.

In other words, raising taxes and cutting government spending while encouraging your population to spend less, save more, and, in addition, providing investment incentives to increase capital spending are recipes for disaster, which, of course, is exactly what many countries are doing. It's called the "paradox of thrift." The combination of tighter fiscal policy, easy money, and a weaker currency, which can work for a small open economy, cannot work for the total global economy. Central bankers should recall that back in the 1990s, the former chairman of the Bank of Japan was indicted as a "financial criminal" for his austerity policies after the Japanese stock and real estate market bubbles first burst. Last week, although I don't think he knows Makin, George Soros chimed in: "What America needs is stimulus, not virtue." He went on to say:

> I believe there is a strong case for further stimulus. Admittedly consumption cannot be sustained indefinitely by running up the national debt. The imbalance between consumption and investment must be corrected. But to cut government spending at a time of large-scale unemployment would be to ignore the lessons of history. What stands in the way is not economics but misconceptions about budget deficits that are exploited for partisan and ideological purposes.

The International Monetary Fund's (IMF) latest missive is not encouraging either. The report argues that the U.S. housing market is poised for another dip down. Home prices have already fallen by about a third since 2006, but the IMF is worried that they are poised for another dip because the tax credits are expiring and one in seven mortgage holders is now at least 30 days late or is already in foreclosure. When a house is foreclosed its price typically falls about a 35% discount, so as foreclosures rise again, they will drag down the entire housing market. With 60% of the average American's net worth in his home, this will have obvious and considerable deflationary consequences.

Makin's outlook, as I understand it, is for a Japan-type outcome (christened Japan-lite) for the developed nations unless we get our act together. In other words, perhaps a decade or longer of sluggish growth with mini-recessions and intermittent deflation of 2% or a little more. He points out that this outcome, while painful, is not necessarily terribly dire. People adopt a "don't buy now because it will cost less later" psychology and the national birth rate falls, but the older generation is not unhappy because holding cash is a very satisfactory investment. The inflation-adjusted, real return on cash is rising and it cannot be taxed. The country's standard of living in real terms remains high. I visited Japan for maybe the twentieth time last June, and you get no sense that this is a gray country suffering through a 20-year depression like the U.S. in the 1930s. Tokyo is alive and vibrant. People elsewhere seem a little sullen but not mutinous. However, Japan's politics are a terrible, paralyzed mess. There is also a Japan-heavy scenario out there, but you don't want to hear it.

If Makin is right, high-grade bonds are going to continue to be great investments. Cash will be king. Equities will be very bad, and the once high-flying retail financial services and mutual fund industries will be disasters. Assets in equity mutual funds in Japan are down something like 85% from their highs of 20 years ago. Real estate also will be very tough. Owning a small business that is profitable and generates cash will be a decent way to survive and enhance the purchasing power of your money. Of course, the risk of social upheaval will increase significantly with the prolonged stagnation and hard times. Think of the 1930s and the rise of Hitler and communism.

So much for ice. Now about fire. Paulson made a speech two weeks ago to the University Club in New York before a standing-room-only audience that overflowed into two other dining rooms. In it, he argued that the U.S. faces double-digit inflation within two and a half years. I wasn't there and the reports of the talk are fragmentary, but 10% inflation by 2012–2013 would be a whopper. His advice was to sell government bonds and buy stocks and real estate. If he's right, the 10-year U.S. Treasury bond now at 103 to yield 2.37% will be yielding at least 10% by 2012, and the price will have fallen from 102 to around 50 or lower.

Inevitably, other shockingly leveraged fixed-income bodies will come to the surface belly-up.

Paulson is an original, daring thinker and investor. I suspect he believes (as do many others) that the great monetarist Milton Friedman was right, and that invariably when the Central Bank prints too much paper, inflation results. On September 10, 2008, just before the collapse of Lehman Brothers, the Fed held $480 billion of securities and that number now has soared to $204 trillion (with a T). With further quantitative easing expected, it's only going higher. "You don't want to own long-dated debt; you want to issue it," Paulson advises.

He went on to say that this is the best time to buy homes in 50 years. "If you don't own a home, buy one. If you own a home, buy another, and if you own two, buy a third and then lend your relatives the money to buy a home. Buying a home with a 30-year fixed-rate mortgage will be a great investment." Other experts point out that houses are as cheap in relation to income as they have been in the 35 years since records have been kept. According to Capital Economics, American home prices would have to rise 11% just to get back to fair value on this measure.

The *Wall Street Journal* also believes that the Fed is going to blunder into an inflationary outcome. In a long and analytical lead editorial last Friday, the newspaper wrote that "there is no such thing as free money, and a second round of QE (quantitative easing) carries enormous risks for what looks to us like far too little benefit." In the Fed's defense, I would point out that there is no evidence that central banks know how to extricate a major economy from deflation, while they have been successful in curing inflation, albeit painfully for the patient. After all, it took World War II to end the Great Depression.

Paulson seems to believe that the "new normal" for the U.S. economy will be around 2% real growth. With his inflation forecast, nominal GDP growth could be 10% or more. He says that, in this environment, high quality stocks with earnings yields of 7–8% and dividend returns in excess of 3% will do well and be much better than bonds. It seems to me that this might be only temporary because, as inflation rises, price-to-earnings ratios eventually will shrink. Investors are not going to be enchanted with stagflation, but Paulson is right that equities will be much better wealth preservers than bonds. Theoretically, dividends should grow with inflation. He specifically cited Johnson & Johnson (3.8% yield), Coca-Cola (3% yield), Pfizer (4%), Citigroup, Bank America, Regions Financial, and Suntrust Banks—a strange assortment. Warren Buffett agrees: "It's quite clear that stocks are cheaper than bonds. I can't imagine anyone having bonds in their portfolio when they can own equities. But people do because of lack of confidence. If they had their confidence back, they wouldn't be selling at these prices. And believe me, it will come back over time."

Paulson loves gold. Over the longer term, he maintains that he can prove that the price of gold has moved with a direct correlation to the monetary base. If the Fed prints more money and doubles the monetary base over the next three years, gold should double also, and he points out that usually, as inflation accelerates, the price of gold goes up even faster than the monetary base. Gold is around $1,200 now and he apparently said if the monetary base doubles again, the formula says gold should hit $2,400 but, in actuality, as investors anticipate more inflation and flee, gold could reach $4,000. Paulson has 80% of his personal assets denominated in gold. He has a gold fund, and he makes no pretense that he is not talking his own book.

So what do I think? Not sure, but I guess, and it is a guess, the most likely case is a less extreme version of Fire and Paulson. Eventually all the paper money that is being printed everywhere is going to create inflation, and, for the politicians and central bankers, inflation is the less painful way out of the malaise. However, in the short run—the next three months to a year—the U.S. and the emerging markets could have an interlude of slow growth in the West, faster growth in the emerging markets, and benign inflation. This combination could cause a cyclical bull market. Sentiment is still incredibly depressed and liquidity is incredibly high. Professional investors get paid for investing, not pining on the sidelines wringing their hands. Remember that about 30% of the earnings of the big U.S. and European multinationals comes from the developing economies.

I feel reasonably good about equity markets right now. The record is that Mr. Market is one of the best economists in the world even though he doesn't have a Ph.D. and is disdained by a profession that takes itself very seriously. The current strength in stocks is very helpful in restoring both consumer and CEO confidence and should produce more retail spending, capital investment, and hiring if it's sustained. However, I admit to not having a strong conviction about the longer-term outlook and the eventual resolution. As investors, all we can do is stay flexible, open-minded, and willing to change as events unfold. I recognize that's not a very helpful conclusion. Sorry!

Miss at Least One Meeting a Day

September was a great month for me, with a gain of 10%, and I added another 3% in October. However, as markets stalled in late October, like a jerk I took off some risk and then I missed another surge in the first 10 days of November and ended up flat for the month. In retrospect it was important to understand how committed the Fed was to more QE if the still fragile economy languished, deflation appeared, and employment didn't continue to improve. Bernanke had intensely studied Japan's nightmare and was desperately afraid of persistent imbedded deflation. He had seen how hard it was to eradicate. Get the big ideas right and stick with them.

Ed Hyman of ISI, the most acclaimed and best economist in the world, in particular emphasized Rogoff's statement that the Fed must make it clear that they were not going to stop QE until they reached their inflation target. This tactic was right out of Chairman Bernanke's book on Japan's lost decades and the failure of the Bank of Japan to use unconventional tools like QE to cure the country's malignant deflation. In the spring of 2012 Paul Krugman in a long essay in the New York Times *raised this issue again, saying Bernanke had not followed his own advice, and on April 26 the chairman responded, saying, "The question is does it make sense to actively seek a higher inflation rate in order to achieve a slightly faster reduction in the unemployment rate?" Bernanke answered his own question: "The view of the committee is that that would be very reckless." I'm a Bernanke fan. Here is what I wrote at the time.*

■ ■ ■

November 3, 2010

Markets around the world have been churning somewhat aimlessly as they await the results of the Fed's meeting next week and the U.S. elections. Anticipation is high. My guess is that markets have discounted a major quantitative easing (QE) announcement

38

and substantial Republican gains, following which everyone expects legislative gridlock. Most investors seem to believe that the September–October rally reflects these two developments. QE is generally viewed negatively. For a chilling review of Chairman Bernanke and QE, see Jeremy Grantham's new letter on the Grantham Mayo web site. I'm a big fan of Jeremy, but not on this one.

The high-frequency economic news continues to be mixed, consistent with the continuation of the "soft patch," but the chances of the dread double dip seem to be diminishing. Emerging market consumer spending is enormous and is now larger than U.S. consumer spending, and emerging market employment is 83% of total employment. The Chinese economy, the second largest in the world, is settling into what appears to be an 8–9% growth track. The developing countries have become powerful growth engines that mitigate the risks as the developed world struggles to recover from the Great Financial Crisis. Meanwhile technology capital spending seems to be improving, and credit spreads are narrowing.

However, Japan is still sick, several European economies look fragile, and some of the developing economies are slowing. The world economy is still perilously close to stall speed. Moreover the persistent softness in the transactions market and the price of U.S. existing single-family homes, particularly when combined with the mortgage documentation furor, is worrisome and by itself could tip the U.S. economy into a double dip. According to the National Association of Realtors, distressed homes, which include foreclosures and short sales, are steadily increasing and amounted to 35% of September home sales. With the documentation scandal and populist outrage burgeoning, this percentage is likely to continue increasing. Typically when a foreclosed house is put on the market, its price falls about 30%, with ripple effects in its neighborhood. The Case-Shiller 10 and 20 City Composite Home Price Indexes have begun to decline again, and the very current ISI house price index is stagnant. A sharp break in house prices with its effect on net worth, confidence, and spending would be profoundly deflationary. Other countries including Australia, Spain, and the U.K. have a similar, although less severe, problem.

My conclusion is that another big round of quantitative easing is absolutely the right move by the Fed. The economist Ken Rogoff put words in Chairman Bernanke's mouth succinctly: "The important thing is to say you are not going to stop QE until you achieve your inflation target." There is, of course, a risk big QE will ignite an inflationary cycle and debase the dollar, but with so much excess capacity of labor and production in the world, a quick jump in inflation seems unlikely, and the economic and social cost of a deflationary-depression "creative destruction"death spiral is too horrendous to accept. Central banks do know how to curb inflation, although the cure is painful. As for the dollar, a growing U.S. economy in the long run is the prime support for the dollar. I think QE is going to work and that the political stalemate in Washington will be resolved with some moderate fiscal stimulus, perhaps in the form of continuation of the Bush tax cuts.

Benign neglect from the politicians may not be such a bad thing, although I would like to see more so-called "shovel ready" job programs and eventually less QE. My view is that after some volatility this week, stocks around the world will begin to go up again (say 10–15%) and sovereign bond prices will fall. Chairman Bernanke wants the stock market to go up and weekly initial unemployment claims to go down!

The record is that Mr. Market is one of the best economists in the world, and a lot of people have now figured that out. Thus a rising stock market could spawn a virtuous circle where the economy does better as both consumers and businessmen regain their confidence and there is more retail spending, capital investment, and hiring. If the Fed succeeds in recreating an inflationary psychology, house prices should first stabilize, the inventory overhang will be reduced, and then lo and behold, they will begin to rise again. In other words we could have an interlude in 2011 of improving economic growth, low inflation, gently rising house prices, 10-year U.S. Government bond yields of 3.5–4%, and continuing earnings gains. With equity investors huddled on the sidelines licking their wounds, massive liquidity, and the need to perform, a mini–melt up could develop. I hope so, and so should the world!

As for me, I have about half of my portfolio in U.S. equities, particularly big-capitalization technology, oil service, and industrials. The quality big-capitalization companies in these sectors are truly multinationals with almost half of their earning power outside America and half of that half in the developing countries. I also own big pharma, some consumer products companies, and the REITs. The other half of the portfolio is in the emerging markets. I like China, Hong Kong, Korea, and Taiwan as high-growth, somewhat cyclical economies and markets. For undervalued, somewhat more risky growth, it's Indonesia, Turkey, and Thailand (particularly the banks). At a conference I attended last week, emerging markets were the favorite equity concentration. A bubble is probably

	P/E Ratios		Price/ Book	Dividend Yield	Price/Sales	Trailing ROE	Trailing Payout Ratio
	2010	12m	Fwd 2010				
U.S.	14.4	12.9	12.7	2.2	1.9%	1.3	15%	28%
Europe	12.4	10.9	10.7	1.7	3.2%	1.0	13%	39%
Japan	14.3	12.9	12.1	1.0	2.1%	0.5	6%	37%
Emerging Markets	12.7	11.7	11.2	2.1	2.1%	N/A	16%	27%
Asian Emerging Markets	13.5	12.3	12.1	2.2	2.0%	N/A	17%	27%

developing, but it ain't anywhere near fully inflated levels. Valuations are not extended—yet. Europe looks cheap, but I can't figure out how to do it. Incidentally, Brazil was the top choice at the conference. I'm queasy.

To wit: The composite of the Institutional Broker Estimate Survey of I/B/E/S's analysts forecasts as of last week are shown in the table.

As always, if events don't work out as I expect, I will change my mind.

Stick to Your Guns

There was a sharp fall in the S&P 500 in mid-November. I was breakeven for the month. In reality there are times to stick to your guns and there are times to cut and run. However you can burn up a lot of performance dancing around trying to avoid wiggles. For once, I was right.

I was tempted to call this piece "Shaking Out the Sissies," but to paraphrase the Bible, arrogant one-liners are dangerous; pride goeth before a fall and a haughty spirit before destruction.

■　■　■

November 15, 2010

Equity markets declined last week, with a steep fall on Friday that has rattled the players. Is this the end of the rally that began in early September? I don't think so, but the pullback could last another few weeks and reactivate the sweat glands. After all, the S&P 500 had briskly risen 17% since late August, and a correction of half that gain is conceivable. I don't believe it's worthwhile to try to time short-term moves of this magnitude because you have to be right twice on the timing (e.g., on both the sell and the buy decision). Tough stuff!

Admittedly there is disconcerting news out there, of which the still-shaky nature of last week's high frequency economic reports is the most important. In the end, the path of the U.S. and global economies is going to determine the ultimate direction of stock prices, and I'm still of the view that we've turned the corner. Time will tell. Meanwhile most of the elite economists and finance ministers around the world are raging at the Fed and Chairman Bernanke and forecasting either failure of QE2 or an eventual inflationary apocalypse. With existing home prices fluttering and another mortgage meltdown looming, I want to ask the critics if they were in Bernanke's shoes, what would they do? It's easy to prescribe creative destruction and a "healthy" deflationary double dip in the abstract if you aren't responsible. However, there is no question that there is a strident, puritanical consensus both in the U.S. and Europe that pain is good for you, particularly if most of the discomfort is going to be endured by other, less virtuous citizens, preferably of other nationalities.

Among the additional issues plaguing markets: the G-20 meeting was uninspiring to say the least (not a surprise), the Chinese are rumored to be about to raise rates (raise rates to combat food inflation?), seasonal factors are supposedly unfavorable (never believed in meteorology), spreads have jumped (true), the lame duck session of Congress could be messy (also true), the Bush tax cuts may not be extended (on the other hand, extension would be bullish), investor sentiment is complacent (really? hedge funds aggressively reduced risk last week), and the funding problems of Irish banks could be contagious. On this last point, painful restructuring of some of the sovereign debt of Ireland, Greece, and Portugal is probably inevitable, but the big one is Spain. There were signs of stress in the Spanish repo market last week, but the bigger Spanish banks are in better condition and will likely be able to rollover debt.

Look! The world is still a chancy, fragile, dangerous place, and investing in equities is a risky business, but what are the alternatives? Cash with a zero rate of return! I still think QE is going to work to raise inflationary expectations and maybe economic activity. Valuation, sentiment, and a continuing gradual economic recovery make equities the asset of choice. The emergence of the emerging economies mitigates but does not eliminate risk. Remember that they are now 35% of the global economy and more like 50% on a purchasing-power parity basis. The Chinese have done an outstanding job of soft landing their economy, and it's ridiculous to postulate that with their social problems they're going to abort their 8–9% growth path. I would take advantage of price weakness in the next few weeks to add to China, Hong Kong, other Asian markets, probably Brazil and Russia, and to the U.S. (tech, oil service, multinational growth, pharma, cap ex), and even some European equities with major business in the developing world. Sell fixed income on strong days.

For important, profound thoughts, google Tudor Investment Company and read Paul Tudor Jones's essay. Paul is the real big thing! He is an incredible combination of thinker, philosopher, trader, but above all a moneymaker. Particularly focus on the last four pages, in which he speculates where the QE liquidity will go.

Stage Two of a Cyclical Bull Market

The beast shakes off its lethargy and I finally get rewarded.

When I wrote to my investors in mid-November, I pointed out that the pleasant Indian Summer rally that began in September had carried 17%, and that a retracement of half of the gains, or about 8%, would not be abnormal, and that shallow corrections, though unnerving, were very difficult to time. You have to get both the sell and then the buy-back decision right. In reality, the decline was only 4%. Now after last week many indexes are on the verge of breaking out above their previous highs, and some, ranging from the German DAX to oil service and industrial equipment shares, already have. Emerging markets, on the other hand, have lagged.

■ ■ ■

December 7, 2010

Last week there were heartening signs of economic strength around the world. J.P. Morgan's November global PMI surveys showed a rise in new orders and employment readings for the second consecutive month, buoyed by turns in China, Korea, and Taiwan. In the U.S., vehicle production, chain-store sales, the non-manufacturing PMI, copper, pending house sales, mortgage applications, and the Beige Book all ticked up, albeit in some cases from depressed levels. Abroad, there were good PMI numbers in Germany, stunning ones in the U.K., and another strong surge in the Chinese manufacturing PMI, to 56.6%.

The doomsayers' consensus keeps saying that China is a bubble full of inflation and the economy is about to collapse, but the bears might bear in mind that the PMI in China had fallen from around 57 in early 2010 to below 51 only a few months ago. Now it is back within a fraction of its earlier high. Not only have the Chinese authorities successfully managed a soft landing in the second largest economy in the world, but they now seem to be establishing an 8–9% growth path. Will this go on forever? Of course not, but China is artfully transitioning from an export-powered economy to one driven more by domestic demand.

I was also heartened by U.S. GDP forecasts being revised upwards by two of the economists I most respect, Ed Hyman of ISI and Jan Hatzius of Goldman Sachs. Hyman is now looking for 3% growth in the U.S. in 2011 and 2012, and Hatzius, who had been quite negative, says: "We now expect growth to remain at last quarter's 2.5% annual rate through early 2011 and then increase over the next year to a 4% annual rate. Core inflation should remain low, at about 0.5% (year to year) through 2012. Monetary policy will remain highly accommodative." Hyman generally agrees, but note that the two came to these conclusions independently. Both stress that underlying demand has strengthened significantly, but neither is predicting a V-shaped recovery.

All I can add is that a scenario of 4% growth, minimal inflation, and no Fed hikes over the next year and a half has not been discounted by the U.S. stock markets. When combined with depressed sentiment and deeply under-invested equity allocations, the combination could be quite intoxicating. A lot of money is poised to come out of bonds and into stocks. Moreover, extension of the Bush tax rates and a less business-antagonistic Obama administration would enhance the cocktail. Hyman points out that in the next quarter, real GDP will probably move above its prior peak in early 2008 into expansion territory. The last nine upswings have lasted 62 months on average, and we are only in the 17th month of this cycle. Sure, this financial crisis and its excesses have been more severe (although the mid-1970s one was no pussycat), but in the past there were never engines like China and the emerging markets accounting for 36% of world GDP.

On the other hand, last week in the U.S. the employment numbers, the Case-Shiller, and average hourly earnings were weak, and admittedly there are still soft spots in some developing countries. PMIs have rolled over in Japan, Brazil, Australia, and Greece. Official interest rate hikes loom in China, Brazil, Thailand, and Chile, among others, because of inflationary pressures mostly related to food. The world is still fragile and vulnerable to policy errors or some other disruption, such as a Korean war, an oil price surge, or a terrorist strike, but that's always the black swan case.

The main dark cloud on the American horizon is not employment (which invariably is a laggard and is bound to improve only slowly) but the housing markets, where 60% of the average American's net worth uneasily resides. The price of existing single-family homes has corrected big time but is still only slightly below its long-term trend line after being far above it for years. I believe in reversion, not only back to the mean, but—after a trip to the stratosphere—to below the mean, and as I wrote two weeks ago, the mortgage documentation fiasco could trigger significant further weakness. Thus the most recent Case-Shiller is disconcerting. However, ISI's weekly survey, which is far more current than Case-Shiller, has ticked up for the last few weeks, although it is still in "the losing-money-at-a-slower-pace" mode.

Another way to observe house prices is by the gross figures. At the peak in the fourth quarter of 2006, the value of houses in the U.S. was $25.3 trillion, and as of the end of the first quarter of 2010 it had fallen to $18.1 trillion and is now probably around $17.5 trillion. Mortgage debt was $10.2 trillion at the end of the first quarter (the latest date for which official figures are available), or 56.5% of value. It is believed that at its peak it was 59.6% of value in early 2009. The shocking realization is that from 1960 to 1990, that ratio ranged between 27% and 29% and was only 38% in 1997 when the great housing bubble began. We've still got a lot of deleveraging ahead of us, and the evanescence of the main component of net worth is not going to boost consumer confidence, which remains in the basement. Chairman Bernanke understands this, which is a principal reason, along with his deathly fear of deflation, that he talked about more quantitative easing (QE) in his interview last Sunday.

Another major event last week came when the European Central Bank (ECB) announced it would buy more bonds. The price of the sovereign debt of the PIGS rose sharply, and their credit default swaps plummeted. However, this is not QE, since Chairman Trichet made it clear that the intervention would be sterilized. I would like to see the ECB launch major QE like the Fed. I recognize that Trichet may not have the consensus among the governors that he would like and needs, but the lesson of history is that in the midst of a financial crisis, central banks should always risk overkill because the eventual cost of not doing enough and having to do it again is so high. I am not a believer in what might be called Christian Science Capitalism, or creative destruction, as it is usually referred to by the hardline advocates of the Austrian school of economic medicine. If the patient has a life-threatening infection and you have powerful antibiotics available, why not use them? Admittedly they may have unpleasant side effects, but they're still better than a trip back to the cemeteries of the 1930s.

The announcements of this morning extending the Bush tax cuts and the additional fiscal stimulus are important positives in that they show that the Republicans and Democrats can compromise to do the right thing, given "the terrain and the situation," as they taught us at infantry officers' school. It looks to me as though Obama is moving towards the center. His willingness to concede on a higher tax rate above a million and propose an inheritance tax of 35% instead of 45% as the left wing of his party wanted is symbolic. Also, the Citicorp sale is a big deal.

President Obama knows that no first-term president who has faced a renomination challenge from within his own party has ever been reelected in modern times. Think of the first George Bush, Jimmy Carter, Ford, Lyndon Johnson, and Hoover. The liberal wing of the Democratic Party is discontented, and the big donors are threatening to keep their wallets closed. If he is going to run (and the story is Michelle is whispering he might not), Obama needs, according to my source, one billion dollars for 2012, and liberals like George Soros have the big money. Thus he has to make the strategic decision whether he is going to tilt their way or move towards the center and rebuild the coalition that elected him in 2008. One swallow doesn't make a spring, but these moves suggest he may have chosen the latter. Unquestionably, a good economy will be a big plus for him.

The global economy *is* improving: Stocks are still the most attractive financial asset, and I don't think it's too late to put money to work in equities and to sell bonds. I think the correction is over and markets could rally another 10–20% in the next few months. This is the second stage of what is probably a cyclical bull market. With some luck and good decisions by the authorities and politicians, eventually it could morph into a secular bull market. For the more conservative investor, blue-chip multinationals with growing dividends yielding 3% or more and substantial free cash flow should be the first choice. For the more adventurous, tech, oil services, banks, and emerging markets, particularly China, are my current favorites. Praise the Lord and pass the ammunition.

The First Word in Analyst Is Anal

December had been a good month for me with a gain of over 5%. Now I was babbling bullishly about prospects at the start of 2011. However, the main thrust of the essay is about the great trader Jesse Livermore and the wisdom of the Old Turkey. Neither one was an analyst. I think it was Livermore who once said, "Analysts write long research reports when they don't have the time to write short ones."

■ ■ ■

December 20, 2010

If the gods of the market ever promise anything, it is a fair guess that for next year they have in mind volatility. I happen to go into 2011 feeling optimistic about the global economy and fairly confident that sentiment, valuations, earnings, and history are supportive of further gains in equities. However, the world and the economic recovery are still so fragile that a black swan event or variations in the high-frequency data can and will violently swing sentiment and markets. Whipsaws are painful for the performance and demoralizing for the psyche. Making money in financial markets in such an environment is about being an investor but also about being a trader. I'm disdainful of the sustainability of prop trading but very respectful of those titans that have the gift and have built huge organizations and fortunes.

The finest trading book ever written is *Reminiscences of a Stock Operator* (John Wiley & Sons, 1994) by Edwin LeFevre. This book is not a "how I made a billion in the stock market" nauseating ego trip or self-serving fiction. Instead it is colloquial reminiscences by a legendary speculator of the mistakes and lessons he learned over a trading lifetime. LeFevre dedicated *Reminiscences* to Jesse Livermore because he was the inspiration and source of the book. In the book, Livermore learns from a wise old speculator named Partridge whom the other traders in the office call the Old Turkey. Basically, Livermore wrote the book. He was the greatest speculator-trader of his era—the first third of the last century. He ran away from home at 14 and arrived in New York with nothing but a smile and a shoeshine and parlayed great instincts and an ability to learn from his mistakes into a fabulous fortune. Livermore was incredibly intense, a student of the rhythm of markets, and was convinced that you had to know yourself and be able to control your emotions to be a successful speculator. You also had to respect and listen to what the market was saying. The most common and usually fatal ailments of the ordinary speculator, he wrote, are greed, fear, and hope. Ironically, his mentor, the Old Turkey, although he was a trader, at times preached a longer-term strategy. The italics in the section that follows are his, not mine.

The game does not change and neither does human nature. And right here let me say one thing: After spending many years on Wall Street and after making and losing millions of dollars, I want to tell you this. *It never was my thinking that made the big money for me. It was always my sitting. Got that? My sitting tight!* Men who can both be right and sit tight are uncommon. I found it one of the hardest things to learn. But it is only after a stock operator has firmly grasped this that he can make big money. The reason is that a man may see straight and clearly and yet become impatient or doubtful *when the market takes its time doing as he figured it must do.* That is why so many men on Wall Street who are not all in the sucker class, not even in the third grade, nevertheless lost money. The market does not beat them. They beat themselves because, although they have brains, *they cannot sit tight.* Intelligent patience! When I was younger, disregarding the big swings and trying to jump in and out was fatal to me. That is about all I have learned—to study general conditions, *to take a position and stick to it. I can wait without a twinge of impatience, I can see a setback without being shaken, knowing that it is only temporary.*

Trading is a hard life, as the prop traders of both yesterday and today will tell you. Livermore went bust several times, and early in his career his relationship with his first wife soured when she wouldn't allow him to hock the jewelry he had given her to meet a margin call. At the peak of his success, he was worth roughly $10 billion in current dollars, and the mere rumor that he was interested in a stock would send it soaring. However, by the late 1930s he was burnt out, depressed by the endless, dogged bear market of the 1930s, and humiliated by losses. In 1940, at the age of 63, he committed suicide in the men's room of the Sherry Netherland Hotel in New York.

The Old Turkey preached: "Don't fight yourself or the market." The human side of every person is the greatest enemy of the average investor or speculator. Identify the big trend and stay with it. Always sell what shows you a loss and keep what shows you a profit, or to put it another way, buy on a scale up and sell on a scale down. It is only what he calls the *semi-sucker* that buys on declines. The first sign of trouble in an aging bull market, he says, is when the groups that had been leaders of the market "reacted several points from the top—and for the first time in many months—did not come back. *Never try to sell at the top*. It is not wise! Sell after a reaction if there is no rally." He goes on: *"In a bear market it is always wise to cover if complete demoralization suddenly develops."*

The Old Turkey does not have—and neither did Livermore—a hard-and-fast rule on when to eliminate a losing position, arguing that the timing depends on the feel of the stock and the market. A drawdown of 10% is about all he will tolerate. It is interesting that it turns out that the other great investor-traders of the first half of the last century, Bernard Baruch, Gerald Loeb, and Roy Neuberger, all followed a 10% rule. Baruch, in his book *My Own Story*, tells how he learned the hard way to cut his losses by selling when a position went against him. "The first loss is usually the smallest. One of the worst mistakes anyone can make is to hold on blindly and refuse to admit that his judgment has been wrong. Occasionally one is too close to a stock. In such cases, the more one knows about a subject, the more likely one is to believe he can outwit the workings of supply and demand. Experts will step in where even fools fear to tread. Never average down!"

An unusually gifted and disciplined trader, Livermore became convinced that the market in the long run was almost always right, and he made sure he was not burdened by too much knowledge of the fundamentals of the positions he took. Thus he was more flexible in his thinking than most of us, who probably over-intellectualize our investments. The great prop trading impresarios of our time have strict portfolio drawdown rules, which are usually set at 10%. Some impose the 10% on the initial equity at the beginning of the year, and some keep 10% at any time during the year. If one of their traders gets down 10% from his high-water mark at any time, he is shut down. I think the latter curb is too severe. A big bull market can survive a number of 10% dips, and the tight rein risks the mortal sin of "losing your position." Having that close a shutdown is like investing with the sword of Damocles hanging over your head. It can screw up your mind. This incident is recounted in *Reminiscences*, where a man named Elmer Harwood has given the Old Turkey a tip, which has worked:

> Well, Elmer made for the old man and, without a word of apology, told Turkey "Mr. Partridge, I have just sold my Climax Motors. My people say the market is entitled to a reaction and that I'll be able to buy it back cheaper. So you'd better do likewise. That is, if you've still got yours."
>
> "Yes, Mr. Harwood, I still have it. Of course!" said Turkey gratefully. It was nice of Elmer to think of the old chap.
>
> "Well, now is the time to take your profit and get in again on the next dip," said Elmer as if he had just made out the deposit slip for the old man. Failing to perceive enthusiastic gratitude in the beneficiary's face, Elmer went on: "I have just sold every share I owned."
>
> But Mr. Partridge shook his head regretfully and whined, "No! No! I can't do that."
>
> "What?" yelled Elmer.
>
> "I simply can't," said Mr. Partridge. He was in great trouble.
>
> "Didn't I give you the tip to buy it?" The tipster always thinks he owns the receiver of his tip body and soul.
>
> "You did, Mr. Harwood, and I am very grateful to you. Indeed I am, sir. But . . ."
>
> "Hold on! Let me talk! Didn't that stock go up seven points in ten days? Didn't it?"
>
> "It did, and I am much obliged to you, my dear boy. But I couldn't think of selling that stock."
>
> "You couldn't?" asked Elmer, beginning to look doubtful himself. It is a habit with most tip givers to be tip takers.
>
> "No, I couldn't."
>
> "Why not?" and Elmer drew nearer.
>
> "Why, this is a bull market!" The old feller said it as though he had given a long and detailed explanation.
>
> "That's all right," said Elmer, looking angry because of his disappointment. "I know this is a bull market as well as you do. But you'd better slip them that stock of yours and buy it back on the reaction. You might as well reduce the cost to yourself."

"My dear boy," said Old Partridge, in great distress, "my dear boy, if I sold that stock now, I'd lose my position, and then where would I be?"

Elmer Harwood threw up his hands, shook his head, and walked over to me. "Can you beat it?" he asked me in a stage whisper. "I ask you!" I didn't say anything, so he went on. "He's made big money and what does he say when I tell him? He says that if he sells it, he'll lose his job. What do you know about that?"

"I beg your pardon, Mr. Harwood. I didn't say I'd lose my job," cut in the Old Turkey. "I said I'd lose my position. And when you are as old I am and you've been through as many booms and panics as I have, you'll know that to lose your position is something nobody can afford: not even John D. Rockefeller. I hope the stock reacts and that you will be able to repurchase your line at a substantial concession, sir. But I myself can only trade in accordance with the experience of many years. I paid a high price for it, and I don't feel like throwing away a second tuition fee. But I am as much obliged to you as if I had the money in the bank. It's a bull market, you know." And he strutted away, leaving Elmer dazed.

I think there's great wisdom in this little vignette. In my opinion, the confluence of events, particularly quantitative easing and the extension of the Bush tax cuts, means that the world is reflating. Maybe it will only work for a few months, maybe it won't work in the long run, but for the time being we are in a bull market for long-term equity financial assets, so don't lose your positions. And listen to the market.

2011

Be Long Term but Watch the Ticks

As the year began, little did I know the horrors that awaited me in 2011. But first there was some good money to be made.

■ ■ ■

This time of year there is always the ridiculous obsession over forecasts of where markets will be a year from now. Mr. Market is smart and sadistic, and he couldn't care less about our calendar. In other words, I have no idea. My sense is, however, that equities are going to work higher in the next couple of months.

As I go into 2011, I'm suffering from a mild case of acrophobia. I've been riding this rally since last summer with a very high net long, and

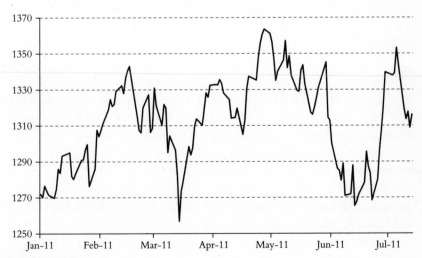

A Volatile First Half

Data source: Bloomberg

markets have had a pleasant, gradual melt-up that has surprised a lot of people. In the U.S., big caps have risen 20% and the smalls are up 30%. Europe and the emerging markets have had roughly similar moves. The question now is whether I should reduce my net long substantially, say to 50 or 60%, and lie in the reeds for a while. As I circulate around, I find that the so-called "smart money" is uneasy and is currently taking off or has already taken off a substantial amount of risk. The prime broker summaries show that, particularly in the last two or three weeks, there has been substantial hedge fund selling of longs and shorts.

"Stocks are clearly overbought," my co-conspirators say. "Bulls make money. Bears make money, but pigs get slaughtered." The bears who didn't participate in the rally are licking their wounds and are reluctant to get involved now for fear of the ignominy of a whip-saw. The pain trade for the consensus would be a further advance early in 2011. I've decided I'm going to hang in there for the time being in anticipation of a further move up in equities in the early part of the year. But I've got nervous feet.

Since we profess to be contrarians, we have done considerable research on sentiment, and on a weekly basis we construct an inclusive sentiment composite that consists of over 20 different indicators. By our measures, sentiment has become considerably more bullish but is not at an extreme. We have found that extremes of bearishness are very valuable timing signals. By contrast, excessive bullishness can persist for a long time without a downward market response. Keynes was right when he famously said that "the market can remain irrational longer than you can remain solvent."

I'm staying invested because the economic news in the U.S.—and for that matter globally—continues to improve. In America, the combination of consumer animal spirits, quantitative easing, extension of the Bush tax cuts, and payroll tax reductions is causing consumer spending, business investment, and job creation to surge. Real GDP growth may reach 4% this year. Regional manufacturing PMIs, First Call earnings revisions, jobless claims, automobile sales, ECRI, and pending house sales all have turned positive. The high-frequency data from the emerging markets, including China, are picking up, and the J.P. Morgan global PMI is rising again. As Morgan puts it: "The drag on global manufacturing is fading." Worldwide, the service sector is returning to life, and consumer and business confidence is rising. Morgan now anticipates that 2011 global growth will be at 3.7%, or 4.5% on a purchasing-power parity basis.

I'm also fairly convinced that there's a big asset-allocation trade brewing for both individuals and institutions out of fixed income and into equities. The mutual fund investor in the U.S. has reacted as he always does. He doesn't sell equities at the bottom; instead he redeems after the first big rally, which is what has been happening for the last 15 months. Institutions follow a similar path. Equity ratios are at record lows, and alternative assets such as private equity, venture capital, real estate, and yes, hedge funds, have been generally uninspiring. The return on cash and short-term paper is almost invisible. We've just finished the worst decade in real terms for equities in modern times, and bonds have done much better for the last 20 years. I believe in reversion to the mean: 6% to 7% real for equities and around 2.5% for 10-year government bonds.

The other big decision is: What are the markets and sectors we should emphasize? I think it's the U.S. and the emerging markets. The European bourses are cheap on valuations, but the Euroland economy still is struggling with its sovereign debt issue and its very serious structural imbalances. The high-frequency data suggest 1.5% real growth (with some possibility of upside) and wide intra-regional variances. Germany is the powerhouse, the soft core of France and Italy stagnates, and the PIGS remain troubled and sickly for at least another year. There is no compelling reason to be involved.

Emerging market (EM) equities have lagged the S&P over the last couple of months because growth and inflation in many of them, particularly in Asia, seem too hot to handle, and as a result their central banks are reacting by raising official interest rates. Thus the near-term ride may be a bit bumpy. This has been particularly the case for the big guy, China, but some of the other EM stars such as Korea, Brazil, India, and Turkey are also hiking rates as inflation rears its ugly head. Although these inflationary pressures are primarily food-related, output gaps have narrowed, and with growth above potential, and still harboring vivid memories of the autumn of 2008, the authorities are reacting peremptorily. Perhaps too peremptorily? Are they fighting the last war rather than the current one? Meanwhile, the currencies of EM countries are appreciating, which is another form of tightening.

Since food prices are a major component of the overall consumption basket in these countries, it is understandable that their central banks are so sensitive. Food prices are around 30% in most in the major EM countries, compared with 15% in the U.S. and Euroland. Yeah, food is important, but I've never quite understood how raising interest rates cures a drought or ameliorates crop failures. Admittedly, monetary policy may have been too stimulative and perhaps has worked too well, but that's not a bad problem to have in a world whose economy is still not out of the recovery ward and where the biggest worry in the major developed countries is deflation, not inflation.

Nevertheless, we are where we are, and the emerging markets may continue to lag U.S. equities coming out of the gate here in 2011. However I'm convinced that being shamelessly fat, the emerging market is the threshold asset allocation decision for the longer-term investor. How much should you have in EM equities and debt? A lot more than you do now! The EM economies are 37% of world GDP but should be 50% in ten years and over 60% by 2030. The EM equity weight in the benchmark MSCI World Index is now 13%, and the consultants estimate the institutions of the so-called developed world have only a 6% weighting in EM equities. At the same time, using a complex model that is a function of growth in employment, capital stock, and total factor productivity, Goldman Sachs forecasts around 5.5% real GDP growth for the ten major EM countries, compared with 2.5% for the U.S. and more like 1.5% for Europe and even less for Japan. EM economies are growing faster because of rising productivity, a faster-growing labor force, higher participation rates, and increasing capital investment per worker.

I think these numbers are about right. It's hard to see with the demographics, participation rates, and the flaccid work ethic of the developed economies how growth is going to exceed these forecasts. However economic growth does not necessarily determine the potential of a country's profits and national stock market. The companies in the S&P 500 derive over half of their earnings from their international businesses, and about 40% of the 50% is from emerging market operations, and that percentage is rising. Over the long run, the S&P 500's real earnings per share growth has been just about the same as real GDP growth. For trend-line future growth, let's assume 2.5% real for the domestic component, 1.5% for the developed international, and 5% for the emerging market part. Overall S&P earnings realistically could trend up at a 3% real rate, which, assuming 3% inflation, translates into 6% per annum nominal. EM earnings growth in line with GDP growth should be about twice as fast, and currency appreciation will add a couple of percentage points a year to GDP growth.

But this is long-term ruminating. For now, I would be about 60% U.S., 6% Europe, and 34% emerging markets. In the U.S., I think it's

	EPS Growth			P/E			Price/ Book	Dividend Yield	Price/ Sales	Trailing ROE	Trailing Payout Ratio
	2010	2011	2012	2010	2011	2012					
U.S.	42.1%	12.9%	13.8%	14.9	13.2	11.6	2.2	1.9%	1.3	15.0%	27.0%
Europe	35.1%	15.1%	12.5%	12.6	10.9	9.7	1.6	3.3%	0.9	13.0%	39.0%
Japan	94.8%	15.0%	12.5%	15.3	13.3	11.8	1.1	1.9%	0.5	7.0%	32.0%
Emerging Markets	31.1%	16.1%	13.7%	12.7	11.5	10.5	2.5	2.8%	N/A	20.0%	35.0%
China	28.3%	14.3%	16.2%	13.8	12.1	10.4	2.3	2.2%	N/A	17.0%	31.0%
Brazil	17.3%	18.0%	11.0%	12.6	10.6	N/A	1.8	2.6%	N/A	14.0%	28.0%

still technology, selective big-cap multinationals with major emerging market exposure, oil services, industrial equipment, financials, and big oil. In Europe also there are some multinationals that have strong emerging market franchises. In the emerging markets, I favor China, India, and the likes of Hong Kong, Korea, Taiwan, Indonesia, Turkey, and Brazil. I have liked Thailand, the banks in particular, a lot but the politics are looking dicey again. The table shows some valuation comparisons, using I/B/E/S analysts' consensus numbers, which should be taken with many grains of salt.

Why do I have quick, nervous feet? Because the economic recovery in the developed economies is still fragile. The piper has not yet been fully paid. Are we really going to get off this easy? The deleveraging process is far from complete. Euroland could blow up. The U.S. housing market is still rickety and choked with inventory. If it continues to free-fall, say hello to the double dip, and the financials will get hit again. A war in Korea or the Middle East would give equity prices a nasty shock.

But if the world holds together reasonably well, equities—while not as cheap as they were—remain the most attractive asset class, and money has to go somewhere. Be an owner rather than a lender.

Shake Well Before Using

I have long been an aficionado of the emerging markets. It may be presumptuous to say, but I was present when they were created as a true asset class.

I still believe but as the chart on the next page shows, emerging markets since 1988 have vaulted over eightfold while the S&P 500 has risen a little over five. Adjusted for risk, volatility, and liquidity, the returns are about equal. Am I just chasing my own tail?

■ ■ ■

January 17, 2011

I believe the most influential, nay crucial, nay magnificent, asset allocation decision for the true long-term investor is the percentage of his or her total equity portfolio allocated to emerging market (EM) equities. By long-term investor, I mean the individual who is thinking about wealth enhancement over a span of two to five years, and the professional who is willing to make a commitment that exposes him or her to considerable benchmark risk. Such a bet could be a make-or-break position, but it's one I have a high degree of confidence in. I despise running money to minimize benchmark risk. We should not be slaves to the usual equity benchmarks, but neither should we be oblivious to them, so my comments take them into respectful consideration.

Let me present some facts. The EM economies this year will be 37% of the global economy and will account for 75% of the world's growth. Goldman Sachs (GS) and the World Bank estimate they will be 50% by 2020 and over 60% of the world by 2030. On a so-called purchasing power basis (PPP), EM already will be half of the world this year. PPP GDP calculates the amount of adjustment needed on the exchange rate between countries in order for the exchange to be equivalent to each

Emerging Markets vs. S&P 500 1/29/88–5/18/12

Data source: Bloomberg

currency's purchasing power. In other words, PPP adjusts so that an identical good in two different countries has the same price when expressed in the same currency. *The Economist* magazine periodically publishes a table that ranks countries on the relative price of purchasing a Big Mac McDonald's hamburger. As of late last year, a Big Mac in the U.S. cost $3.71 versus $6.78 in Switzerland, $5.26 in Brazil, and $2.18 in China.

Using a complex model that is a function of growth in employment, capital stock, and total factor productivity (faster-growing labor force, higher participation rates, and increasing capital investment per worker), GS forecasts a 20-year compound annual growth rate (CAGR) of real (in other words, inflation adjusted) GDP in local currencies of around 5.5% for the 10 major EMs. This contrasts to a 2.5% CAGR for the U.S. and more like 1% to 1.5% at best for Europe, Germany, and Japan.

Here are the International Monetary Fund's, GS's, and my back-of-the-envelope 20-year CAGR forecasts for the major EMs: China 6.5%, India 6.4%, Philippines 5.9%, Malaysia 5.4%, Indonesia 5.1%, Turkey 4.8%, Brazil 4.6%, Mexico 4.4%, Thailand, Israel, South Africa 4.3%, Russia 3.8%, and Korea and Taiwan 3.5%. Since the less mature EMs will even grow faster, the EMs as a group will have CAGR of real GDP over the 20 years of 5.7%. By contrast, the developed economies will chug along at 1.8% per annum, producing total global growth of 4.1%. If these forecasts are right, we will all live happily ever after.

Nevertheless, as we know, 20-year projections are horse manure sprinkled with heroic assumptions, and I don't necessarily agree with some of these country growth rates, but presumably they were scientifically derived as described above. However, it's the magnitude of the difference between the developed economies and the EMs that is so overwhelming . . . and compelling!

Developing country currencies have tended to appreciate versus the dollar, the euro, and the yen as higher productivity drives convergence towards PPP exchange rates. Over the long run, this trend should add anywhere from 50 bps to 250 bps per annum to the increase in the EM's real U.S. dollar GDP. Obviously, currency appreciation is also an important plus for investors who own EM equities!

Unfortunately it's not GDP progress but earnings per share growth that drives stock prices. Over the long run, the real earnings per share growth of the S&P 500 has been on occasion less than real GDP growth, although in the last 25 years it has been pretty close. Today the S&P 500 derives slightly over half of its profits from its constituents' international businesses, of which roughly 40% of that 50% is from EM operations. For the future, let's assume CAGR of 2.5% real for domestic S&P earnings, 1.5% for other developed economies' profits, and 5.6% for the EM portion. Presumably the share of the great U.S. multinationals' earnings coming from EMs will be rising in the years to come. All this translates into a little over 3% real for overall S&P earnings, which with 3% inflation (a guess!) would be 6% nominal. The EM's nominal earnings growth could be 10% to 12%.

GS also models using market-cap-to-GDP ratios, which I think is a little silly. So much depends on the degree an economy is privatized. In any case, here are the numbers. GS invented the term BRICs (Brazil, Russia, India, and China). GS maintains that they are the big-GDP, big-population, big-potential EMs, and they currently represent a little less than half of the total GDP of the EMs. Observe what happens by 2020.

	Current			**2020 Forecast**		
	GDP ($)	**MKT CAP ($)**	**MC/ GDP (%)**	**GDP ($)**	**MKT CAP ($)**	**MC/ GDP (%)**
U.S.	14,614	13,850	95	18,065	22,398	124
China	5,633	4,716	84	15,694	16,417	105
BRICS	10,906	8,292	76	25,854	25,244	98

Source: Goldman Sachs Economic Research

How about valuation? Do EM equities already reflect this optimism? As of last week, according to the I/B/E/S consensus estimates, EMs as a group are trading at 11.5 times forward (next 12 months) earnings, the U.S. is at 13.2 times, and Europe is at 10.7. On price-to-book, a more stable, tangible measure of value, the U.S. is at 2.3 times, EM at 2.1 and Europe at 1.6. Admittedly EM equities have been discovered. There was a substantial flow of mutual fund money into them last year. But exploited and overvalued, already a bubble? I don't think so. They still look very cheap to me. Sure they may be the next big bubble, but in a world awash with liquidity and bubble-prone, you want to be there in the inflating stage.

The consultants say the average developed world institution now has 6–7% of its total equity portfolio in EM. The EM equity weight in the MSCI World Index by which almost everyone is evaluated is now 13%. EM equities are grossly underweighted in this index, as they are 31% of world market cap. Considering that the EMs are growing about twice as fast as the U.S., probably four times as fast as Europe and Japan, and will be at least 50% (and maybe more) of the global market cap of equities in less than a decade, why wouldn't you want to have at least 20% to 25% of your equity portfolio in them right now?

How would you accomplish this? One way is to own large-capitalization, developed-market multinationals. This class of stock is as cheap relative to the rest of developed market equities as it has been in many years. Yields range from 2% to almost 4% with low payout ratios, growing dividends, and reasonable free cash flow valuations. However, owning them is not direct involvement in EM, and their mature developed markets businesses are a drag. Their managements are not exactly entrepreneurial. However, they are a nice, safe way to get exposure. Think of McDonalds. Yields 3.3%, 27% five-year dividend growth, 48% payout ratio, 16 times trailing earnings, and it has proven its franchise is internationally very viable.

Direct participation is trickier. EM hedge funds have been disappointing. Too many of them have underperformed the indexes, and their fee structure is a burden. The big, long-only managers have also struggled versus the benchmarks. Investing directly in the EM indexes is frustrating because you end up being heavily weighted in the "discovered" markets that have done well rather than in the frontier, undiscovered ones that will be the big future winners. Last year, the already beloved BRICS seriously underperformed the rest of the EM universe. Owning index funds and the major exchange-traded fund, EEM, presents the same problems. ISI says there are 158 non-BRIC EMs.

The big winners in the EM space in the years to come are the "frontier markets" that have minuscule market caps today and are poorer and riskier. For example, Nigeria, which has a chaotic reputation, also had huge oil reserves, 180 million people, and improving politics. Vietnam, known for corruption and beleaguered with inflation, has 100 million people with 90% literacy and a young, rapidly growing workforce. Mobile phone penetration (an excellent future growth measure) is soaring. Then there is Rwanda and Bangladesh, currently World Bank favorites. Maybe even Pakistan, Iraq, or Venezuela. Ethiopia's GDP grew 8.5% last year.

I don't know whether there is more risk in EM or developed equities. The two secular bear markets of the last decade show there's a lot of volatility in both. In the end, I conclude that the intelligent investor should have substantial positions in the great multinationals for both underpriced quality and EM reasons. In addition, he or she should have 20–25% in EM equities, half of which should be indexed (Vanguard, Fidelity, etc.) and the other half actively managed, either in-country ETFs, with a long-only manager, or by stock picking if you are adventurous and have the resources. Own a frontier fund!

The famous bank robber Willie Sutton late in his storied career was hauled up before a judge. Willie had already served two terms for holding up banks. The judge viewed him sternly from the bench and then leaned forward and asked:

"Tell me, Mister Sutton, why is it you always rob banks?"
"Mister Judge," Willie replied. "It's simple. Because that's where the
money is."

Why as an investor do you want to own EM equities? Because that's where the growth is.

Fancy Dinner and Candlelight

February 2, 2011

*W*ell here we go again! Despite the potentially destabilizing consequences of Egypt and scary house price numbers in the U.S., equity markets are humming today. The latest batch of economic numbers around the world continues to confirm an unfolding and powerful broad-based business and household spending recovery. The PMIs released in the last few days were very strong and in some cases at 20-year highs. And it's not just the U.S.! Across Asia, from Taiwan and Korea to Indonesia, ISMs and the high-frequency data are rising. Japanese consumer durable spending is growing at a double-digit rate, and global auto sales, amazingly, are now 10% above their pre-recession high of four years ago. Even Europe is looking better.

It could well be that the focus for a while is going to be on the U.S., the S&P 500, and technology (the QQQs). As fourth-quarter 2010 profits came in above expectations, analysts are revising their earnings estimates upwards for the S&P 500. For the full-year 2011, $92 to $95 a share is not inconceivable, and with the consensus real GDP forecast for 2011 around 3% to 3.5% with the nominal up perhaps another 300 basis points, fevered imaginations could be talking about over $100 next year. With ten-year Treasury bonds yielding around 4% to 4.5%, this combination could spark a run into the neighborhood of the old highs.

But this could be pie in the sky. I still have this uneasy feeling that the proverbial piper has not yet been fully paid. Are we really going to get off this easy? Am I just acrophobic? I'm still about 90% net long and inclined to ride this tiger at least for a while longer.

I suspect equities in the U.S. are rallying so fiercely because the fast money is still underinvested and chomping at the bit to get back into the game but wants to buy on dips. Sadistic old Mr. Market is delighting in not giving the boys much of a chance. We had a sharp one-day Egypt-oil correction last Friday, and over the weekend I heard much mumbling that it was the beginning of the end. The correction was over after a couple of hours on Monday.

The last two weeks I was traveling in Europe. One evening I attended a dinner in London in one of those paneled, ornate rooms with fine food, candlelight, and portraits of distinguished ancestors above the fireplaces. Present were 17 other aggressive investors, both hedge fund and long-only people, some attired elegantly and others looking as though the next event was a night out with the gang. As we went around the room, the few bullish participants were apologizing and appeared embarrassed. Apparently it isn't fashionable to be talking bullish after the sustained run we've had since last summer. The bears at this dinner were articulate, passionate, and had glossy coats and profound reasons ranging from Chinese real estate to an economic double dip and the sovereign debt crisis spreading to America, the U.K., and Japan.

Almost everyone pointed out that the market is "over-bought," whatever that means, and that sentiment indicators such as a number of strategists positive and market-letter advisory services were almost all bullish extremes. As I discussed a month ago, we systematically track U.S. sentiment. We have found that extremes of bearish sentiment are valuable and valid timing indicators to which attention should be paid. By contrast, bullish extremes are a blunt instrument.

In the U.S., I still love technology. Ten years after the last Internet-related capital spending cycle in tech peaked, a new cloud-related technology surge with different players is underway, and it could last three to five years. Also as I have preached to no avail, big capitalization, high-quality multinationals are as cheap compared with everything else as they have been in 50 years. As the great Lee Cooperman of Omega puts it, "They are the best houses in a bad neighborhood, and if the world's okay, they're the best houses in a good neighborhood." I would add that they're not going to make you rich, but they will make you richer! I like great global franchises with 3% plus dividend yields that are growing. I've owned energy and the oil service stocks, but they've had a big move, and I'm wondering. Small-cap and low-quality stocks as classes are expensive.

What am I watching and worried about? The data last week on the U.S. market for existing single-family homes were dismal. Prices have started to fall again, and the inventory of unsold units continues to grow. Government supports have expired. After their mammoth bubble, they've fallen 25% but are only back to their long-term trend line. Another 10% down could be coming. With 60% of the average American's net worth in his home, the retirement age going up and Social Security and pension payments coming down, won't even the fabled, often delusional American consumer ponder saving more and spending less?

Clearly Chairman Bernanke has belatedly figured this out, even though he was a co-conspirator with Greenspan in blowing and promoting the bubble to begin with. He actually reassured America back in October 2006 that "the U.S. housing market has never declined." However, now he has got religion, and QE2 is all about flooding the system with liquidity and getting asset prices up. Under current circumstances, it's the right thing! Since his Jackson Hole speech, he has succeeded magnificently with the stock market, which is very important for confidence, capital spending, and, eventually, employment. Now he must end the bear market in housing or a double dip in the economy with whiffs of inflation could happen. The struggle is underway.

Also I worry that the global economy is still fragile and vulnerable to a black swan or a policy error by the Authorities. The Asian central banks are raising rates and reserve requirements to fight food inflation, which I don't think is a good idea. Europe still has not dealt with its sovereign debt crisis, although there is a new rumor every week. It needs to.

I'd love to believe that we are in a new, long-term secular bull market, but it's a stretch. If what we have is a cyclical bull market in the trading range, it's getting long in the tooth. Stay tuned.

Stevie Cohen Tells a Good Story

Early February 2011

According to the latest Bank of America Merrill Lynch Fund Managers Survey, economic growth, inflation, and central bank rate hike expectations are "creeping" higher. Equities and commodities are the assets of preference, and both are at record over-weights. Even more interesting, 5% of fund managers admit to being over-weight emerging market equities as compared with 56% just four months ago. On the other hand, U.S. equities are the most over-weight macro call, at 34%, and European equities have risen from minus 9% to plus 11% over-weight.

As you would expect with this backdrop, the respondents have become negative on and are selling fixed income. As for sectors, according to the survey, tech is very hot, and banks are recovering. The tech underweight has risen from −21% to −7%, with an even bigger swing in European banks from −56% to −16%. Defensive sectors like pharma, utilities, and the consumer staples are unpopular. I've followed this survey for years, and it's good, systematic stuff. However, you can't be a crazed Pavlov dog type of contrarian because, as I've mentioned, sentiment works much better at bottoms than at tops. Sometimes you even have to be a contra-contrarian. As I wrote last week, I'm a believer that emerging markets are due for a big bounce.

Today I went to the ISI conference in New York and listened raptly to Paul Tudor Jones interview the legendary Stevie Cohen of SAC. Jones, another icon, could also be a stand-in for Charlie Rose. Cohen was formidable, fascinating, and relaxed, considering the scrutiny he's under. Understandably Jones didn't ask him about the SEC problems of his former associates. SAC is huge, but nobody knows exactly how huge— certainly in the low teens of billions. Fee structure is also shrouded in mystery. The rumor is 0 and 50. In other words, no fixed fee and half of the profits. Perhaps apocryphal and maybe 2 and 25, or 30, is more likely.

Over the years, performance has been spectacular, although SAC apparently was down 18% in 2008.

The firm has 100 portfolio managers and 150 analysts. They report to 10 sector heads. The firm closely monitors the PMs' hit rates, with the best averaging about 55% and the worst around 48%. The key is whether they make big money when they are right and lose less when they are wrong. Stevie wants good, big ideas. SAC is an intense investment factory. Each week starts with phone interrogations Sunday afternoon, and he listens and cherry picks the best ideas.

When you have a big idea, he said, make a significant bet of 10% and make it quickly. Good ideas get circulated very fast these days. He figures it takes about 20 days for the alpha from an idea to get disseminated. He uses charts for entry points, but fundamentals override technicals. He used to be, he said, much more of a trader. Now he thinks in terms of intermediate-term (three- to six-month) gains. Don't fuss with your winners, and spend most of your time on the positions that aren't doing well and listen to what the market is telling you. There are always people out there who know more than you do, and he implied that a position that didn't act well got liquidated quickly. However, he said he didn't think in terms of stop-loss limits. He thinks the three things that can kill your business are leverage, excessive concentration, and illiquidity.

Jones asked him what he thought about markets now. He's very bullish on stocks. He really likes the way the U.S. market grinds higher relentlessly with low volatility. If volatility increased a lot, he would get nervous. His two best ideas, he said, were tech and China. The tech theme is both hardware (communication, mobility plays) and software, by which he seems to mean stuff like Facebook, Open Table, Groupon, Twitter, etc. As for China, he has come to believe that the Chinese consumer is going to come on strong much faster than people believe. If so, not only will the Chinese economy make a successful transition from being export-driven to domestic-demand, but Southeast Asia overall, and maybe even the world, will benefit. That last sentence is my interpretation and me (loaded up on China and Asia) talking, not him.

If SAC continues to thrive with its incredible size and exorbitant fee structure, it will be the story of our time, and Stevie Cohen will be of comparable stature to Buffett as one of the two or three greatest investor-managers. I think I understand how Buffett does it. Cohen's process to me seems like black magic. If it all sounds too good to be true, it probably isn't true.

The Canary in the Coal Mine?

February 10, 2011

*E*merging markets (EMs) topped out last fall and bumped sideways through the end of last year. Since then the index has dropped about 9%. This damage isn't too bad in absolute terms, but versus the S&P 500, EM has quite dramatically underperformed since October as the chart on the next page shows. The index line has fallen further than shown in the past day.

As the second chart indicates, over the long run these vicious potholes in EM relative performance versus the S&P have occurred fairly regularly although the current one is quite severe. The chart is also interesting in that it shows that on a relative basis the EM index is back to the same level it was at in mid-2007. I still believe that since the developing world is where the growth is and since its valuation by most criteria is lower, in a bubble-prone world awash with liquidity, eventually EM will be the bubble of all bubbles. Just for the record, at the end of last week based on analysts' consensus, bottoms–up 12-month forward earnings estimates EM was at 11.2 versus 13.5 for the U.S. and 11.1 for Europe.

As I've written previously, the principal reason for this fade is investor fear that EM central banks are still early in a tightening interest rate cycle because of rising inflation. However, I did not expect the reaction to be this severe. The biggest cause of this inflation is soaring food prices as shown in the third chart. What a spike! The index is up 64% from its low last year! Steadily growing demand has violently collided with restrained supply and the speculative momentum money has jumped into food commodities. Food is between 20 and 45% of the family budget in the EM world compared to 10% or a little less in the developed economies, so the EM's vulnerability is obvious. I am skeptical of the potency of higher interest rates in curing crop failures and droughts.

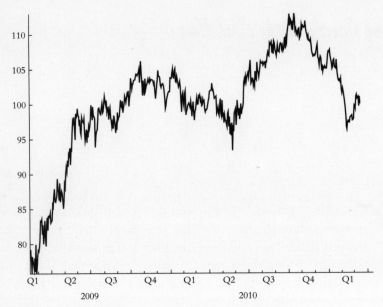

MSCI Emerging Market Index (USD) vs. S&P 500

Source: MSCI, Standard & Poor's Corp. Traxis Partners LP

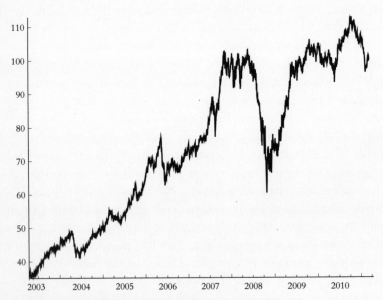

MSCI Emerging Market Index (USD) vs. S&P 500

Source: MSCI, Standard & Poor's Corp. Traxis Partners LP

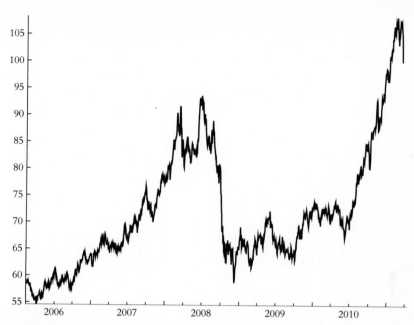

Blended Goldman Sachs Commodity Index Food, Livestock and Agriculture Index

Source: Standard & Poor's Corp. and Goldman Sachs, Traxis Partners LP

Admittedly, certain central banks in EM countries may be somewhat "behind the curve," and monetary conditions are loose. Output gaps are generally in safe territory. There are upticks in core inflation and some overheating although only India and perhaps Brazil have severe overheating. There is also asset inflation in certain countries, most notably in Chinese real estate. In the past, EM investors haven't reacted to overheating until there were large current account deficits and inflation was in the high-single-digit range. Brazil, India, and Turkey have current account deficits.

The weakness in EM stock prices has intensified in the last two weeks as momentum-oriented foreign investors who last year poured money into the EM space as though there was no tomorrow have fled like a herd of wildebeests. Seven billion dollars was redeemed out of EM equity funds last week alone.

The total shares outstanding of the iShares Emerging Markets ETF have fallen 21% since mid-November. Meanwhile, the media and strategists have discovered the EM inflation problem. Yesterday it was a *Wall*

Street Journal front-page story, and subsequently a congressman held up the *Journal* and seemed to accuse Chairman Bernanke instead of the weather of being the creator of food inflation. In other words, we must be close to the point where the EM inflation scare is the consensus wisdom, which would suggest that a lot of the problem has already been discounted.

Now let's look at a couple of the markets that have been hit hardest. These charts show the performance of Brazil, China, and India not versus the S&P 500 (which would show much steeper falls) but versus the falling EM index overall. The first of the three charts shows how Brazil has been hammered. Among its problems are inflation, a slowing economy, rising bond yields, an overvalued currency, and central bank tightening; however, it's at 9.8 times forward earnings, 1.7 times book, and yields 3%. My beloved China's ailments have been discussed ad nauseam, but bear in mind it's buffeting at 11.7 times earnings and 2.3 times book. Not bad for an economy that should grow 8% to 10% this year. India's problem is inflation, corruption, and valuation (it's still the most expensive EM at 14.5 times earnings and 3 times book).

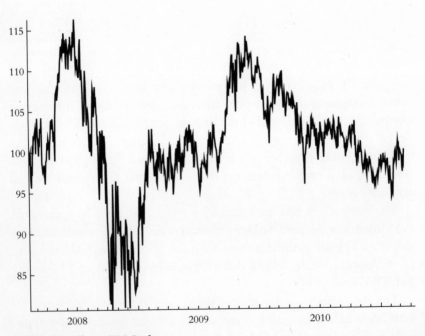

MSCI Brazil vs. EM Index

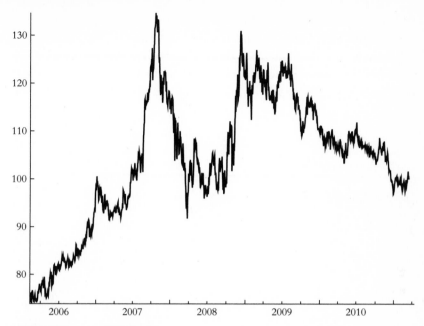

MSCI China vs. EM Index

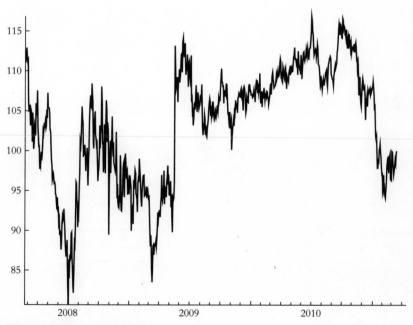

MSCI India vs. EM Index

Source: MSCI, Traxis Partners LP

What's my conclusion? The EM underperformance and liquidation has reached extreme levels and the disconcerting rise in inflation has been pretty well discounted. Regime change in Egypt is not a factor. For investors it certainly is too late to sell EM, and it's probably time to start buying.

Still Hanging in There

March 9, 2011

Very tough times to run performance money! Rumors about the doings of a madman in the Middle East swing oil and the S&P and can make you look like an idiot in a nanosecond. However, the core difficulty is that the so-called intelligent investor can make an equally rational case for this roller coaster being either a bull or a bear. I've still got a lot of risk on, but I'm apprehensive. Warren Buffett early last week said he saw big opportunities, and he had an "itchy" trigger finger on his elephant gun. I've got an itchy finger on my eject button.

The bull case is that the U.S., European, and even the sickly Japanese economies are enjoying an impressive broadening and deepening recovery that is rapidly transitioning from a snap-back to a true expansion. Global PMIs show that both the industrial and service sectors are booming and that confidence, capital spending, and hiring are rising. Earnings estimates are still being increased, and based on the I/B/E/S consensus numbers (which are probably low), the U.S. is at 13.4× 12-month forward estimates, 2.3× book, and with yields at almost 2%. The same numbers for Europe are 11×, 1.4×, and 3.3%, and for the emerging markets, it's 10.9×, 2.0×, and 2.2%. Sounds okay to me.

Where else are you going to put your money? Fixed income yields are close to historic lows, and with higher inflation at some point almost a certainty, the capital loss risk is high. Farmland? Looks as though a bubble is brewing. Private equity? Too illiquid, long lockups, and the bloom is off that rose. Real estate is the same story. As for liquidity, there is still a huge amount of institutional and public money on the sidelines or sulking in bond funds. Could stocks have another 10% move up from here? Sure!

I suppose commodities are an alternative, but they're not in my circle of competence. And they're not an investment. An investment by definition is either current income or a stream of future income. When you buy a commodity you have to be assuming that you are going to be able to sell it a higher price to someone else because it has no income. Thus it is not investing—it is speculating.

The dark side of the moon is that my worries have doubled. Three weeks ago, I was principally concerned about the price of single-family homes in America and the sovereign debt crisis in Euroland. Since then, the latest data on home prices and the inventory overhang, etc., have deteriorated again. A new low in prices looms. As for the European sovereign issue, the prime ministers and central bankers continue to fiddle the same old sour music while Rome smolders. Let's pray that at the summit meeting later this month they get their act together. Restructuring the debt and austerity will be painful for the PIGS and will require sacrifices from Germany.

The two new plagues are the oil price and the risk of a major policy error from premature tightening. I have no special insights on Libya, Saudi Arabia, or the Middle East, and I learned long ago that nobody knows anything about oil, but it is obvious that the risk of oil going to $150 or higher has increased. By now everybody knows much higher oil prices could derail the global economy, so the effect of revolution and supply disruptions in Saudi Arabia would sky oil prices and sink stocks.

On the other hand, the consensus may be exaggerating the power of oil. The world's energy intensity has declined enormously in the last 30 years. The global economy uses 40% and 75% less oil per unit of GDP compared with 15 and 30 years ago. History shows that early-cycle surges in oil price have less of an impact on growth, and strategic and industry reserves are much larger now than they were at the onset of earlier crises. Furthermore oil-price surges redistribute wealth to developing countries, which are far bigger global consumers than they were in the late 1970s. That said, the best economist in the world, Ed Hyman of ISI, said just recently that if "Brent goes to $130, we'll probably cut our GDP forecast from +3.5 to +2.5." That's not trivial.

The other worry that has emerged is a policy error in the form of premature monetary tightening. Some of the Asian central banks have already started to hike rates, but their economies sailed through the recession. Last week Jean-Claude Trichet said the European Central Bank (ECB) may raise interest rates in April to combat rising inflation. The global recovery is too fragile, particularly with oil prices rising, for this kind of foolishness. Trichet is worried about headline inflation. Bernanke cares about core, and he said it right: "Increases in gas prices are very troubling for a lot of people . . . but they are not inflation per se. Inflation is an increase in the overall price level, which is very low." I believe that serious inflation in the West is not going to happen as long as unit labor costs and wage rates are not rising, which they aren't.

So I'm inclined to hang in there. My biggest positions are U.S. technology stocks (QQQQ with a few deletions), China (H shares, Hong Kong, and Hong Kong property), the oil service stocks, and the U.S. financials (Wells Fargo, Citigroup, et al.).

The Market Is a Discounting Mechanism

E quity markets have snapped back today, but the environment is still fragile and incredibly volatile. My inclination, although a little bloody, is to continue to hang in there pretty fully invested. There's too much panic and radiation misinformation floating around to sell. I have added a substantial position in both the Nikkei index and the Japan ETF EWJ.

I'm not sure, however, if we are out of the woods for good. Bahrain is in serious trouble, and any unrest in Saudi Arabia that threatened oil production would justifiably terrify global financial markets. In addition, the latest data on U.S. existing single family home prices showed another 3% decline to a new low, and the fundamental data, particularly the huge shadow inventory, are very disturbing. New housing starts also have plunged, and the three-month average is on the verge of a downside breakout. Although the high-frequency data show the U.S. economy is steadily strengthening, the recovery remains delicate and vulnerable to a shock. Europe is no healthier, and the sovereign debt issue is not resolved although some progress was made last weekend.

My bet is that after a steep near-term decline, the Japanese economy comes on strong in the late summer and first quarter of next year. They are tough, resolute people and they will get their act together. Thus unless the Bahrain or house price black swan flaps its wings, the world is going to look okay for a while and stocks will have another move to the upside. I remain intrigued with the emerging markets, particularly China (FXI), India (INP), and Brazil.

The events in Japan are going to cause central banks to be much more circumspect about tightening. In addition, as the first chart shows, food prices are coming off the boil. The fall in rice prices is particularly encouraging. Inflation remains dormant.

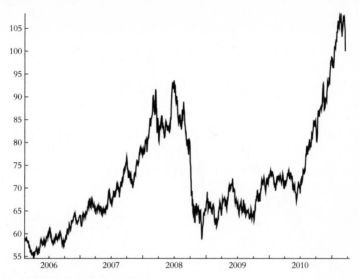

Blended GSCI Food/Ag Index

Source: MSCI, Standard & Poor's Corp., Traxis Partners LP

The second chart shows the anemic rally emerging markets have had versus the S&P 500. The next charts shockingly display the underperformance of China, Brazil, and India versus the emerging markets index. In effect, you are looking at double underperformance.

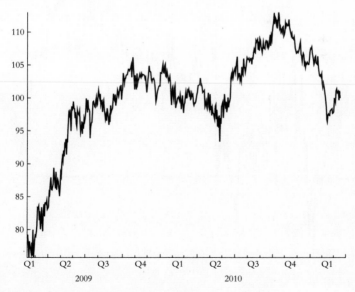

MSCI Emerging Market Index (USD) vs. S&P 500

Source: MSCI, Standard & Poor's Corp., Traxis Partners LP

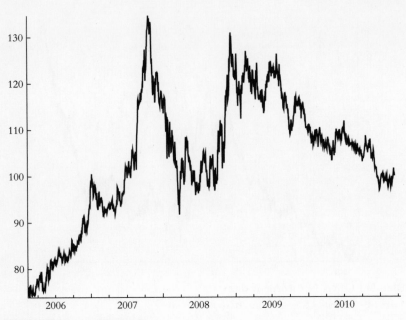

MSCI China vs. EM Index

Source: Standard & Poor's Corp., Goldman Sachs, Traxis Partners LP

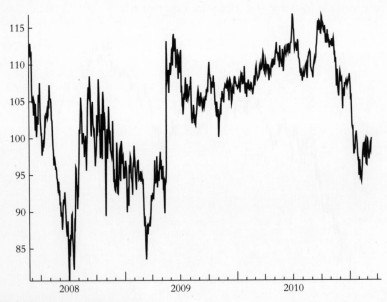

MSCI India vs. EM Index

Source: MSCI, Traxis Partners LP

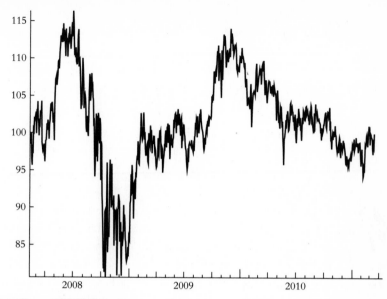

Brazil vs. EM Index

Source: MSCI, Traxis Partners LP

The Madness of Crowds

March 28, 2011

*M*arkets are sometimes very smart and perceptive, and this particular market acts "well"—an expression that is often and reasonably mocked as naive. Does this market know something we don't? Maybe. I'm very respectful of the collective wisdom of crowds and a stock market is a crowd of investors. Please bear in mind that I am talking about crowds—not mobs. A crowd becomes a mob when it morphs in a disorderly fashion into greed, violence, and vulgarity and succumbs to emotional contagion. The etymology of mob is from the Latin: mobile vulgus. It is not crowds, but mobs, greed, and excessive liquidity that create bubbles.

Present-day equity markets in the face of earthquakes, revolutions, wars, and governments that fiddle while Rome burns continue to lurch ahead and are now generally only a couple of percentage points below their mid–October recovery highs. A great many people are angry, frustrated, and scratching their heads as to why, and there's still a lot of money on the sidelines. The ISI hedge fund index is down from 55 to 51, and the American public continues to redeem both U.S. and emerging market mutual funds.

The financial intelligentsia is very disdainful about the intuition of markets. Much has been disparagingly written about the insanity of markets. The great classic is Charles Mackay's *Extraordinary Popular Delusions and the Madness of Crowds* (Broadway, 1995), which is religiously stacked in every professional investor's bookcase. Its most famous lines are: "Men, it has been well said, think in herds. It will be seen that they go mad in herds, while they only recover their senses slowly, and one by one." Friedrich Nietzsche wrote, "Madness is the exception in individuals but the rule in groups," and Thomas Carlyle famously said, "I do not believe in the collective wisdom of individual ignorance."

In the investment world, even the mention of "the crowd" has an intensely pejorative connotation. You don't want to be part of the crowd because the crowd is stupid and always wrong. Avoid "crowded trades at all costs" has become a hedge fund maxim. "Be contrarian!" They assume the market is dumb and manic. Of course at times parts of it are. However, instead I would argue most of the time you should respectfully "listen to the market."

Hayek wrote of "tacit knowledge." Tacit knowledge is knowledge that is intuitive to individuals or is derived from a particular place, job, or way of life. Since it is intuitive and instinctive, it can't be easily summarized or communicated; and in fact people who have it may not even know they have it. Yet is very valuable because it reflects the deep life experience of human beings dispersed over the world. A stock market, so the theory goes, in its totality is this information and knowledge aggregated through the price mechanism into a single number that reflects all these hopes and fears and judgments. It was Napoleon Bonaparte who said "the only one who is wiser than anyone is everyone."

What is not appreciated is that when asked or required to make judgments independently and in a rational way the record of crowds is impressive. James Surowiecki in his book *The Wisdom of Crowds* (Anchor, 2005) cites a number of examples of the rather amazing collective wisdom of a large number of people making serious, individual bets about everything from elections to the number of jelly beans in a jar. The uncanny record of the Iowa Electronic Markets is an example of the first and the famous contest where the average of 800 guesses of the weight of an ox at an English country fair was within one pound (1,197 versus 1,198).

In more reflective moments I would argue that the stock market is a wise and farseeing old thing. Its wisdom is not on little things, but it has tacit insights on the ebb and flow of great events. It consists of a very diverse, motivated, engaged, reasonably intelligent crowd. Just the fact that they have sufficient money to be investors suggests there is some natural selection process at work. Its record during the civilization-threatening times of the 1930s and 1940s is very impressive. In March of 2009 when even the best were profoundly negative, markets realized the global economy was turning.

So what could the markets be sensing now. Obviously I'm just guessing, but here are a couple of scenarios. The first is that the global economic recovery is more broadly based and self-sustaining than the conventional wisdom grasps. Could real GDP by the late summer be growing at over a 5% rate in the U.S. and close to 4% in Europe. If so, corporate profits will comfortably exceed expectations—perhaps 100+ for the S&P 500. The developing economies already are in rude health. Overall growth of this magnitude would set in motion a series of virtuous circles. Meanwhile with so much excess capacity in both labor and industry, inflation will only be creeping higher and the 10-year Treasury bond might be yielding less than 5%. Couldn't the S&P sell at 15 to 16 times earnings under these circumstances and be making a run at the old highs?

Another scenario is that the revolution in the Middle East is a great event for the world. Corrupt, inefficient dictatorships that enriched themselves at the expense of the people are being replaced by democracies that eventually will create shared growth, a rising standard of living, and eventually huge new consumer markets. These revolutions of the Arabian spring may be comparable to the fall of the Berlin Wall and the transformation of Eastern Europe from autocratic communism to semi-democratic capitalism. Of course this won't occur overnight, and it will be slow, ugly, and painful but, it is fundamentally bullish. Furthermore it is possible that the new messy democracy and the spreading of wealth and prosperity will diminish the appeal of terrorism and defang al-Qaeda and the Taliban. People who can vote, have jobs, and see opportunity for themselves and their children are not inclined to blow themselves up or so the theory goes. Listening to the Sunday morning talk shows, none of the great and the good pontificating foresaw anything good happening from the Arab spring.

Third, investors are looking through the S&P 500 and the big European indexes and saying the big companies that dominate them are really global profit machines not mired in the mature, slow growth, developed economies. Sure, the U.S. may have a new normal of 2–3% real GDP growth, but something like 53% of the S&P's earnings come from outside the U.S. and of that amount a rising 30% derive from the emerging markets. The developing countries already are almost 40% of global GDP and growing three times as fast. Furthermore, their currencies are likely to be appreciating versus the dollar and the euro as higher productivity drives convergence towards purchasing power parity exchange rates. Thus the trend-line earnings growth for the capitalization weighted indices could be 6–7%.

Who knows? All these rosy scenarios are probably romantic, tacit pipe dreams. There are some very frightening black swans flapping out there. Their names are Sinking American Home Prices, Deficits, Too Much Leverage, the Middle East, and Europe's Festering PIGS. Then there's the voice from the clouds that keeps repeating, "you can't get off this easy; the piper still has to be paid." Of course we have to keep a close eye on these ugly birds but for the time being I'm listening to the market.

Earthquakes and Equities

April 12, 2011

There are many complexities in the present predicament of the markets. It's a very difficult conundrum to unravel, and there is no point in recounting the various deadly and benign crosscurrents, headwinds, tailwinds, and black swans. It does seem that the fog and clouds over financial markets have darkened in the last week or so, and what Ed Hyman calls "a negative feedback loop" has developed. The Middle East smolders, the price of oil goes up, gasoline prices climb, headline inflation rises, central banks (notably the ECB) tighten, the dollar falls, so oil goes up again, and the vicious circle continues. This combination of expensive oil and central bank tightening is negative for the global economy and the recovery, and some, but certainly not all, of the most recent high frequency data suggest a softening. If oil continues to work higher, stocks aren't going to like this mixture, and the charade in Washington on Friday certainly doesn't help.

However, I suspect that the elevated oil price is mostly about the Middle East in general and Bahrain and Saudi in particular and not about excessive global demand growth. There is plenty of supply and large inventories. My bet is that the next move in oil prices is down $10 to $20 a barrel and not up, so I'm not selling stocks. I'm also not brimming with conviction and I'm, as they say, light in my loafers.

On another more ethereal subject, I continue to be intrigued by Japan and the Japanese stock market. The experience of Japan over the last 20 years demonstrates how dangerous it is to allow deflation to take root in an economy burdened with a massive load of private debt that the debtors are desperate to pay down. The Bank of Japan and the ruling party's errors compounded the deflation and a psychology of "don't buy now; it will cost less later" became entrenched. Prices inexorably fell, and paralysis of the economy and the political system ensued.

However, the earthquake damage and the nuclear disaster constitute an enormous supply shock to the Japanese economy as electric power is rationed and ruined production facilities are shut down. Japanese companies have been deleveraging by paying down debt, and loan demand has been nonexistent, but now companies are going to have to borrow money to rebuild. The earthquake should activate loan demand, and production shortages should narrow the output gap and maybe even trigger some inflation.

I'm not into mysticism, but there is a mythology in Japan that the major earthquakes that have haunted and rattled Japan for centuries have presaged major cultural and social changes in this island race that is so inbred and isolationist and whose culture is utterly unique. The 1855 Tokyo earthquake that leveled the city marked the beginning of the end of 200 years of isolation and a complex, rice-based feudalism with the emperor ruling from Kyoto called Tokugawa or Edo period. It was followed by a Japan more industrial and open to the world, and that fought and won a great sea battle with Russia. The 1923 quake signaled another new age with the rise of aggressive militarism and an obsession with Asian conquest that culminated in World War II. Ironically the Morgan banks took the lead in underwriting large sovereign debt issues that financed the rebuilding and rearming of Japan. The emperor two decades later remembered this assistance and was reluctant to go to war against the U.S. because of it.

Some Japanese who believe in this theory even argue that the devastation from the atomic bombing of Hiroshima and Nagasaki was like an earthquake and signaled the end of that tragic, militaristic era. They also maintain that a half century later the Kobe 1995 quake signaled the end of the postwar industrial boom, and heralded 20 years of recession and deflation. They maintain that in the decade after earthquakes the legend is that the Japanese birth rate dramatically rises. As we all know, Japan's declining population and workforce have been a huge drag.

It is not that earthquakes cause or bring change in and of themselves. Instead they signal change. The Japanese island, the earth, the tectonic plates are speaking. The land is an integral part of the race, the nation, and the Japanese believe its adherence to cultural and racial purity causes its superiority. Think of the thousands of years when Japan and the Japanese were totally separate from the rest of the world. Even today immigration is restricted and blocked. Read *Shogun* or the modern history leading up to 1941.

The Japanese are a formidable race. After the 1923 earthquake they determined to build the best navy in the world. Their naval academy, Eta Jima (EJ), made Annapolis look like a summer camp for privileged teenagers. The EJ midshipmen were tutored by English instructors in table manners and making toasts. They were told they must always travel first class and must never be seen carrying packages. The academic, physical, and seamanship programs were very demanding, and above all unswerving loyalty to the emperor, obedience, and readiness to die in battle were instilled and enforced. Surrender was never an option, and captains went down with their ships.

The midshipmen were also brutalized. The smallest infraction of a rule resulted in a beating and guard duty punishment. Every Sunday freshmen stood at rigid attention in the yard for four hours and were slapped and pummeled by upperclassmen. The physical training program was intense and unrelenting. British offices observing the curriculum questioned whether it didn't produce narrow-minded robots whose creativity and independence had been beaten out of them. Despite its Spartan regimen, Eta Jima had 30 applicants for every one accepted.

Throughout the Imperial Navy, violence was employed to enforce discipline and blind obedience. Just as the samurai warriors of the past could kill an impudent commoner who failed to get out of their way in the road, a Japanese naval officer in 1941 was required to strike five times with his fist any enlisted man who failed to salute or who disobeyed a direct order. Petty officers on Japanese ships carried thin, but heavy, sticks called "spirit bars" with which they hit enlisted men who did not respond fast enough to orders. It is now accepted that by the late 1930s the Japanese had the best, most sophisticated navy in the world with three super battleships and five aircraft carriers. The U.S. just got lucky in the crucial battle of Midway in 1942, and in addition, an operations officer on the Japanese flagship allowed his aircraft to be caught on the deck refueling. Incidentally he had gone to Princeton instead of Eta Jima.

The Japanese army was as arduous as the navy. Soldiers were expected to be able to walk 35 miles a day for weeks on end with full pack and equipment. They were conditioned to endure on a diet of rice and water and four hours of sleep a night. Young officers were trained to be aggressive and always attack. In fact, their field manual had no chapter on retreat. Japan had also developed an aeronautical marvel, the Zero, which was the fastest, most maneuverable fighter plane in the world. Ironically, the Zero was delivered from its factory by ox cart.

It all seems a little farfetched, but it is conceivable that the effects of this earthquake are analogous to "creative destruction" and could kick-start the lethargic Japanese economy and end the long period of stagnation. Its consequences could also revitalize the political and corporate governance process that has once again demonstrated the overwhelming incompetence of the prime minister, the bureaucrats who really run the country, and finally the careless and pathetic management of the major electric utility whose president had an emotional collapse.

This is all very existentialist and mystical. So many words have been written about Japan, but the truth is "nobody knows nuthin'." There are some truths though. First, the Japanese are a formidable and serious race and they will not become extinct. Second, Japanese equities have experienced one of the longest, most severe secular bear markets in history (look at the chart). Third Japanese equities are very, very cheap. The market sells at about book value and at half of sales. From a technical perspective, the short-term chart looks interesting, too. Following the earthquake I bought a 10% position after the first big decline, sold half of it on the bounce, and now am wondering if I shouldn't buy it back.

Portrait of a Secular Bear Market

The Riddle of Japan

May 2, 2011

The fund had a decent April and we are now up 4.5% net for the year to date, but performance was somewhat disappointing. The gain for the month should have been bigger. We got the direction of the market right and ran a healthy net long, but our country and sector picks were mediocre. Our substantial tech basket was our leader closely followed by the smaller Morgan Stanley basket of European companies with significant emerging market exposure. As discussed in an earlier report, we added a customized tech basket of a small group of individually selected technology companies that are primed to benefit from the developing environment of tablets and so-called cloud computing. Thai stocks and our substantial positions in the Thai banks were another bright spot. Our timing in buying Japan after the earthquake market break was rewarded, and we subsequently added as our confidence that strong growth will be evident by the fourth quarter grew. Other holdings across Southeast Asia (particularly Korea) were helpful.

Unfortunately, the China stake and our Hong Kong luxury holdings did very little and were flat for the month. We still believe Chinese economic management is misunderstood, and that the market is too cheap. Agricultural commodity prices are coming down, and the tightening cycle may be closer to having run its course than investors think. We actually lost money in the global oil service stocks and in U.S. financials, which we liquidated mid-month. The continuing decline in existing single-family home prices for the time being eliminates the possibility of loan portfolio write-ups. Our short in U.K. commercial real estate cost us money but could have been worse. We continue to run a high net long as the U.S. market grinds higher. As we have noted before, this slow, low-volatility melt-up is a good sign.

The Federal Reserve's Real Broad Dollar Index which is much more encompassing than the DXY has broken to a new low, and with various headwinds from weather, Japan, higher oil prices, and inventories buffeting it, the global economy seems to be tipping back towards a new soft patch. So why are stocks going up? In the U.S. the reason is fairly clear. First quarter earnings reports have been generally spectacular, and the Fed is still creating liquidity. Bernanke and the people that matter at the Fed (Yellen and Dudley) apparently believe that core inflation rather than headline is key, and that the combination of the continuing decline in house prices and strong commodity prices are deflationary because they sap consumer disposable income. If there is a global soft patch, presumably oil prices would decline, which would be helpful. However, the nightmare for the Administration and the Fed would be an interruption of Middle East production and higher oil. Then we would have stag deflation.

I agree with them. Real wages and salaries declined in March −0.1% but real transfer payments rose enough to cause a slight rise in real disposable personal income. The U.S. economy is still convalescing and fragile. The president and presumably Bernanke know that no first-term president in modern times has been reelected with unemployment above 7.5%. My view is that QE3 is becoming more likely, and that as long as investors think the soft patch is temporary, it's bullish. With all the crosscurrents around the world, trying to catch moves in themes, countries, sectors, and currencies is tough stuff. I've done nothing new with my portfolio except to add to my Japan position. Central bank tightening and Japan's problems have weighed on Asia but I'm still a believer. Korea might be a little ahead of itself, but China, Hong Kong (luxury property), Thailand (banks), and Indonesia could be poised for a run.

The dictionary definition of a "loser"—that most disdainful of all epithets—is "a person, team, country, etc. that consistently loses." Ironically after being the world champion of "winners" for over 30 years, in the last 21 years Japan and the Japanese stock market have become synonymous with "losers." In this article I will attempt to make the self-serving case that Japanese equities could be poised for a reversal of the great secular bear market that began so long ago. Once again I return to history to bolster my case that the Japanese are a formidable race, and that Japan and its market will not just endure but will prosper. Considering how cheap Japanese stocks are, if that is a correct assumption, in the face of a Mt. Fuji of bad news, the long-term investor has to be interested.

Japan's stock market is still down 65% or so from its 1989 high. The rally from the 2008 bottom has been half of that in the S&P 500 and even less against the emerging markets. For over 20 years Japan's economy has stagnated and been plagued with deflation. The price level as measured by the GDP deflator has fallen 10% since 1990, and at one point commercial real estate quotations were off almost 90%. In this hostile environment, Japanese banks, which in the late 1980s were the wonders of the world with enormous market capitalizations, suffered even more enormous loan losses, and Japan Inc. has been humbled as it lost its cache.

The fall from grace of the equally revered Japanese management style has been equally stunning. Too many trophy assets ranging from Van Goghs to Pebble Beach and Rockefeller Center were top-ticked on leverage, and Japanese companies stumbled as profit margins shrunk, labor was used inefficiently, and they became increasingly bureaucratic and lost their innovative edge. The fabled "salary man" is now a worldwide symbol of pathetic ineptitude. The governing and political processes also have become subjects of derision. Prime ministers have come and gone every six months, and the Diet debates endlessly but does nothing. Another prime minister who has bungled is about to go.

In the midst of all this unpleasantness, the birth rate of the country has declined sharply, and by 2005 the total population of Japan and the size of its workforce were falling. One study maintains that Japan is the only country that had more pets than children, and the U.N. projects the working-age population over the next 40 years will fall from 81.5 million to 51.8 million. *The Economist* recently chimed in, warning that these demographic trends inevitably would doom the country to lower GDP growth, a reduced standard of living, and a smaller tax base, making its swelling public debt a crushing burden. Implied was the threat of demographic extinction. I would note that demographic extrapolations have a nasty habit of being misleading. After World War II in which Japan lost three million men, the Japanese birth rate, particularly of boys, mysteriously rose sharply.

Admittedly real GDP progress is a function of growth in the workforce and productivity. If female participation in the workforce reached U.S. levels, 10 million jobs would be added. Seventy percent of Japanese women quit working after their first child as compared to 30% in the U.S., so there is huge potential for a rise in the female participation rate. However, presently recent college graduates, both male and female, are having a very tough time finding jobs with over half of last year's class without work.

The bears on Japanese stocks and government bonds (JGBs) delight in terrifying people about the world by reciting the argument which has been around for years that Japan's ratio of public debt to GDP is 227%, and that it is more than seven times the government's revenues. Lower debt levels have forced defaults elsewhere in the world, notably Russia in 1998, and Portugal and Greece are in dire straits under similar circumstances. If for whatever reason the interest rate on JGBs rose 200 bps, J.P. Morgan calculates debt service costs on the debt would absorb the entire revenues of the government. However, it should be noted that the 227% figure is on the gross debt, which excludes the government's large foreign exchange reserves. Net debt is an unhealthy but not catastrophic 114% of GDP. Nevertheless as the following table shows, Japan gross financing needs are far worse than anyone else's.

2011 Gross Financing Need

	Maturing Debt	Budget Deficit	Total Financing Need
Japan	48.9%	8.9%	57.8%
United States	18.1	9.7	27.8
United Kingdom	7.5	8.1	15.6
Spain	11.0	6.9	17.9
Germany	9.1	3.7	12.8
France	16.0	6.0	22.0
Portugal	15.5	5.2	20.7
Greece	16.5	7.3	23.8
Sweden	4.5	1.4	5.9
Australia	2.0	2.5	4.5
Ireland	6.1	11.8	17.9
Italy	18.2	4.3	22.5

Edward Chancellor of GMO has published another of his wonderful essays, this one about Japan, entitled: "After Tohoku: Do Investors Face Another Lost Decade from Japan?" In it he makes the following points:

1. Ninety-four percent of JGBs are held by Japanese individuals or institutions, not foreigners. Nations don't default on debt held by their own people.
2. Sovereign debt defaults often are also caused by economic contractions in countries that are locked into an uncompetitive exchange

rate. Japan, unlike the PIGS, has its own currency, controls the Bank of Japan, and could devalue if necessary.

3. Japan has a large current account surplus. CA deficits are dangerous and go with defaults.

4. Japan could raise taxes. The tax rate and the consumption tax are low, and tax revenues are only 30% of GDP compared to 40% in Europe. Personally I feel raising tax rates now would be a mistake. The solution lies in more growth and inflation—in other words, a rise in nominal GDP.

5. The bears' claim that a 200-bps rise in the interest rate of JGBs in a few years would bankrupt the government is erroneous. No, says Chancellor, if interest rates rose because inflation and growth increased, tax revenues would increase sharply.

A new negative is that the major Japanese companies such as Toyota are now saying they want to diversify more of their production (and that of their suppliers as well) out of earthquake-prone Japan. Perhaps in the future the Japanese stock market will have an additional risk premium attached to it because of this earthquake factor. Some even argue that whereas in the past there was a major earthquake every 40 or 50 years, climate change is shortening the cycle; for example Kobe was only 26 years ago. Why would you invest in a country that has a huge natural disaster every 20 years or so? You wouldn't if you believed it.

There is no question that the tsunami and the quake delivered a huge shock to the Japanese economy. The best economists I follow are saying that business activity in the next couple of quarters will be much weaker than predicted even a month ago. Consumer confidence has plummeted, and retail sales in March slumped 8.5%, the biggest drop in 13 years. Cannon, Toyota, Honda, and Sharp have recently again revised down their 2011 guidance. The Nikkei News this weekend had a cheery story: "Japan Airlines May Be Entering a New Ice Age." Presumably businessmen and tourists will stop flying to Japan for fear of being quaked. Belatedly, S&P piled on downgrading its outlook on Japan to negative and estimating that reconstruction costs were likely to reach as high as 50 trillion yen ($62.6 billion). Electric power shortages this summer could further set back the recovery.

As I wrote previously, there is a mythology in Japan that the major earthquakes that have haunted the land for centuries have presaged major cultural and social changes. The land and the sea of the sacred home islands were speaking to the people. Each one—going back to the 1855 quake, to 1923, the atomic bombs in 1945, then Kobe in 1995, and now 2011—bookended an era. The spirits of the tectonic plates are speaking. It's time for a change. The message on this quake is that Japan has to get its act together. It must reform its dysfunctional political system, the crushing bureaucracy that stifles innovation, revitalize the birth rate, and perhaps even its antiquated social system. Certainly this quake has delivered a tremendous supply-side shock to an economy desperately needing to be jolted out of stagnation and deflation.

My guess is the Japanese economy will come back strong late in the year. The Japanese are a proud and formidable people. They believe their culture is the best and most sophisticated in the world. A long succession of victories over the centuries have convinced them of their invincibility and racial superiority. I just finished re-reading *Sea of Thunder* (Simon & Schuster, 2006) by Evan Thomas, a wonderful history and naval story but also a study of the mentality of the Japanese race, particularly at the end of World War II.

The Japanese from the late 1920s on embraced a suicidal, expansionist militarism that engulfed even the emperor. In the last days of the war when it was obvious that all was lost, Japan sent its super-battleship *Yamato* by itself without any air cover out on a suicide mission to attack the American fleet. The great ship, the most powerful in the world, was manned by 3,100 cadets and students that didn't even know how to operate the fire control system of the anti-aircraft guns. The *Yamato* never got near the U.S. ships and was sunk by carrier-based airpower with a loss of all hands. The book tells of how when the ship left, port young midshipmen were given lengths of rope so they could lash themselves to the ship as it began to flounder. In the spring of 1945 thousands of young Japanese died in *Kamikaze* missions, and even after the atomic bombs, the Japanese people pledged to die resisting the American landings. "One hundred million deaths rather than surrender" was the popular slogan. It's no wonder that Truman decided he had to use the atomic bomb.

Then the Emperor spoke on the radio. Most Japanese had never heard his voice before. He told them Japan had unconditionally surrendered and they must peacefully abide by the terms of the Potsdam Declaration. They "must endure the unendurable." Then he said he had written a poem. It was customary for the emperor to communicate his most sincere emotions through such 31-syllable *tankas*.

> Courageous the pine
> That does not change color
> Under the winter snow
> And truly the men of Japan
> Should be a forest of pines.

His coded message was that the Japanese people were like the forest pines and the American occupiers were the winter snow causing a temporary whiteness of the pines. However spring would come and the snow would melt and be gone. Japan, however, was like the trees. It would be strong and green again and become a great forest. Suddenly the mood changed. Resistance ended.

In the event when the American troops landed they were astounded by their docile reception from the Japanese people. One Marine's diary tells of the advance Marine regiment moving down a street in Yokohama in a column of files with slung but loaded M-1s and fixed bayonets.

> Japanese civilians and soldiers lined the route of march. They stared but showed no animosity or emotion. Their faces were ashen and their expressions blank. They surprised us by courteously bowing low as we passed. They were quiet and docile. Was this the vicious, brutal, fanatical enemy that we had fought for so long. How could this be possible?

The American occupation of Japan was the most successful in history—before or since. Resistance was almost nonexistent.

My laboriously made point is that the Japanese people are capable of sudden and dramatic changes, and that the country may be once again be about to transform itself. One of the benefits of having a totally homogeneous culture and passionate racial pride is the ability to get the entire nation moving simultaneously in one direction. As Chancellor points out, Japan modernized at a blinding pace after the Meiji restoration in 1866. In the 1925–1945 period the surge was in the wrong direction while in the postwar era in one glorious stampede Japan doubled its national wealth per capita in a world record 20 years. However, note that I am talking about long-term trends, not the next month or so.

Everyone has heard *ad nauseam* and to no avail what great value Japanese stocks are. When looking at these ratios bear in mind that Japanese companies have cash holdings equivalent to 30% of their market capitalization. The entire market is probably selling at a significant discount to replacement cost book value. So what? Japanese stocks have been cheap for years. Here are the current I/B/E/S numbers. When you look at the raw statistics, Japan doesn't seem that undervalued considering how screwed up it is. That's why I concentrate on the long-term secular revival case. If Japan could get its ROE up into the low teens and sell at one times sales you could make a lot of money. Ending stag-deflation and generating some nominal GDP growth is the key. That's why the earthquake could be a game changer.

	P/E 12 Months Forward	Price/ Book	Div. Yield	Price/ Sales	Trailing ROE
Japan	12.4	1.0	2.1%	0.5	8%
U.S.	13.0	2.3	1.8	1.4	16
Europe	11.8	1.7	3.2	1.0	14
Emerging Markets	10.6	2.1	2.1	N/A	17
Emerging Asia	11.9	2.3	1.9	N/A	17

I own Japan (and the yen incidentally) through EWJ, which is the iShares MSCI Japan Index Fund. You could also buy futures in either the Topix or Nikkei 225 Indexes. Then there is MSJNUSDX on Bloomberg, which is a customized basket of the blue chip Japanese exporters. When you own EWJ you are long the stocks and the yen. I don't expect to make money from the yen portion of the trade but I don't think the yen will weaken much if the Japanese economy begins to snap back.

Start Buying the Dips

My hip had been giving me some trouble, but by now it was killing me, and I was agonizing on whether to cancel my June trip to Asia. However, that's no excuse. I missed the first warning signs of problems and trouble to come.

■ ■ ■

May 1, 2011

It seems to me the events of the last couple of weeks are mostly bullish not bearish for global equities. Fears of rising inflation whether core or headline have been an increasing and strengthening headwind for both developed and emerging markets. Particularly in the developing world, central banks have been tightening, but with negative real interest rates, most still remain behind the curve. Investors are worrying there is a lot more to come, although it was interesting that old fox, Jean Claude Trichet, said the strong euro presently argued against further ECB tightening.

At the same time whether because of bad weather, the Japan earthquake, or the Arab Spring, economic growth around the world has been slowing, and almost everyone is forecasting a "soft patch." Government debt markets seem to think a "double dip" is not completely out of the question. How else to explain the rally in Treasuries? The hottest technician now says his favorite long is the 10-year Treasury bond.

What equity markets want is sustainable growth with low inflation. They don't want yet to hear about central bank tightening! Thus the decline in oil, metals, and agricultural commodity prices was good news as was last Friday's better employment report even though there were a few caveats. However, the steepening fall in the price of existing single-family homes in the U.S. and the bulging inventory statistics are worrisome. I try to rationalize them by arguing that the weather was lousy in March, and that sales don't usually pick up until spring. Also believe it or not, Dr. Copper and Dr. Kospi (Korea) still have a big following, which to the bears confirms a more serious slowdown.

The bad news is that the new stumbles and stress in Europe are an ongoing and growing negative. Europe's story is too much debt and too little growth. Greece is insolvent and slipping backwards in terms of its economy, fiscal reform, etc. Delaying the solution means the cost of saving the country is inexorably increasing, and Portugal and Ireland loom in the background. Meanwhile the EMU economy is sagging again.

There are two obvious solutions, both extremely painful. First, the IMF and the European Union have to give Greece more money. Second, the maturities on their sovereign debt have to be voluntarily extended by the lenders. It's euphemistically called "sharing the burden." Ultimately a 50–75% haircut, however disguised, is the only solution. But the damage to the ECB, European banks, and the Greek banks themselves is appalling. A 50% haircut would leave Greek banks with equity only 1% of assets.

Thus I'm still not attracted to European equities as an asset class, although I do have a basket of European companies with a high percentage of their earnings from the developing markets. In fact, the basket was my best performer in April. I'm still big in U.S. tech, both the old champions and the new contenders. The former are just too cheap at below S&P valuations in relation to their above average, albeit reduced growth prospects. Recently I listened to a revered value investor expound on the once-in-a-generation opportunity to buy the likes of Cisco, Intel, Microsoft, IBM, et al.

The new tech centurions playing around in the cloud and remote are not as cheap but their growth rates and potential are much more exciting. Nobody believes that companies like Apple, Qualcomm, and VMware can keep growing so astronomically and I don't either, but at 13 to 14 times the next 12 months' earnings playing around in the cloud and remote, all they have to do is grow 15–20% annually to be compelling investments. I also continue to hold, despite the turbulence, energy-related names ranging from Exxon to Schlumberger. I believe! The industrial machinery, capital goods stocks look like buys again, and small-cap value ETFs make sense.

I wrote about Japan last time so I'll spare you that. In the emerging markets the tightening of fiscal and monetary policy as both core and food inflation ticked up have been a wet blanket. I really haven't changed my focus from Southeast Asia—China, Hong Kong, Thailand, Indonesia,

Korea, and Taiwan. I particularly like Hong Kong luxury property plays and the Thai banks. Chinese stocks are a mighty beast waiting to be aroused by the first signs of the end of tightening and the easing of inflation.

I sense international investors are struggling with how to invest in the EM. Traditionally, long-only Asian funds have done poorly, and hedge funds, which are often nothing but proprietary traders, have also under-performed the indexes. Country and specialized ETFs have a built-in, small inherent lag but in my view are the way to go.

In summary, buy the dips.

Babbling Away

F inancial markets are looking sickly again because of an accumulation of weaker global economic data over the last two weeks and because of the dark cloud of European sovereign debt. I suppose you could say that America's inability to create a credible deficit reduction agenda is another ominous omen. Global industrial production has slowed from over 9% to somewhere around 2% currently because of adverse weather, the sudden recession in Japan, related supply chain interruptions, soaring gasoline prices, and an inventory swing. Furthermore, a number of the developing economies, particularly China, have been tightening fiscal and monetary policy. In fact, the Chinese PMI released over the weekend tipped markets into the sharp drop we saw on Monday.

The bears are talking of global growth remaining at this low level for some two or three quarters at best, in other words, another prolonged soft patch, with a double dip and whiffs of deflation not inconceivable. In fact, with the 10-year Treasury bond approaching 3%, clearly a lot of fixed income investors buy the latter scenario. Equity investors argue stocks, since the lows have had a big run and profit margins are unsustainably high so earnings forecasts are going to transition from being too low to being too high. Reversion to the mean it's called. The end of QE2 is cited as another negative, and they mutter gloomily about the inventory of repossessed homes causing further pain in house prices. Incidentally, I worry a lot about this one, too.

I don't believe the prolonged soft patch story. I think this is a temporary hiatus and that the U.S. is still in a self-sustaining, albeit moderate, economic expansion. All the production negatives cited above are dissipating, and the employment picture is slowly but steadily improving. Corporate profits and balance sheets are very strong, and capital spending is rebounding. The latest senior loan officers' survey indicates a recovering propensity to borrow. With the fed funds rate virtually at zero, bankers are regaining their commercial instincts. Fed policy is extremely stimulative with an expanded balance sheet.

As for China, the authorities have slammed on the brakes, for which I give them a lot of credit. Real growth is slowing, not stopping. There may be one or two more tightening moves. The Chinese economy is currently cranking along at 9.2% real GDP and they probably want to get the pace down to 7%. Nonfood inflation was 2.8% in May and food inflation is moving lower. If that's not a soft landing, I don't know what is. At a recent China conference, I'm told, the investor chatter was all about a hard landing and major earnings declines. The government's risk profile may be switching from worrying about too-hot inflation to too-low growth. Don't forget China is the second biggest economy in the world. The third biggest, Japan, has fallen further than initially anticipated but seems to be bouncing back faster and real GDP could be expanding at a 4% rate by the fourth quarter. Toyota is a good leading indicator, and they just announced they have ramped up production.

Don't underestimate the Japanese people's ability to adapt to a new environment. For decades I suffered in Tokyo summers in formal, dark, gray woolen suits and with head colds from frigid office air conditioning. Now I hear this summer the environmental agency is mandating air conditioning being turned down or off and that sports shirts, Bermuda shorts, and polo shirts are the dress code. I still like the market.

If my case is correct, investors should hang in there through this turbulence. To trade a correction in a cyclical bull market you have to believe the correction is going to be at least 10%. As of this morning, the S&P 500 is down 4.5% and emerging markets about 9%. Could the S&P decline another 5–7%? Yes, if the high frequency economic data continue to be soft. Do we think we are on the precipice of a new cyclical bear market? No! Equities are still slightly undervalued and with interest rates where they are, sentiment depressed, and massive amounts of central bank liquidity being added, eventual higher inflation makes fixed income unappealing. Spreads have sunk.

One of the biggest anomalies in the present equity markets and particularly in the U.S. is the undervaluation and poor performance of large, high-quality stocks. I find it fascinating and perplexing. It seems to me in a world where cash and currencies are so volatile, subject to speculative manipulation, and have no yield, that this class of stocks is an attractive alternative. After all, they are highly liquid even in large size, represent a diversified call on real earning assets around the world, and have a yield of 2.5–3%. Whenever investors have lost faith in paper, gold has always been the leading alternative, but its value cannot be determined by analysis, it has no yield, and is burdensome to transport and hold. Gold mining stocks and gold exchange-traded funds are another medium but have specific problems and risks. What kind of stocks are we talking about? World-class multinationals that have franchise dominant positions, Petrobras, Vale, and Itaú Unibanco are Brazilian examples.

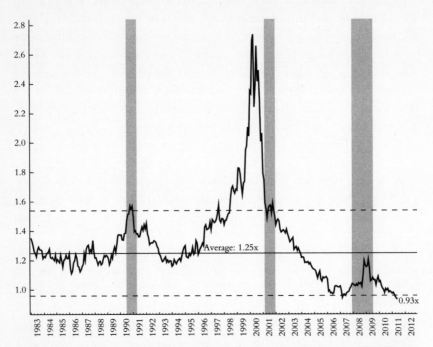

Composite Relative Valuation Indicator: Top 50 Stocks vs. the Rest—Overdone Reversion to the Mean

Swensen and Yale

For a large pool of money, whether you're trying to get richer or preserve and enhance wealth, getting your asset allocation right is what the battle for investment survival is all about. I am talking about the objective of fiduciaries—true investors, not speculators—and make no mistake, survival means generating "good real" (inflation adjusted) returns over time. What does "good" mean? Answer: Real returns of 6% to 7%. Bear in mind that in real terms over the 20th century, equities in the U.S. returned 6.7%, Treasury bonds 1.6%, and Treasury bills 1.1%. Swedish and Australian stocks did even better but a lot of markets such as France and Italy generated considerably lower but still positive returns. There are no solid numbers for the equities of the developing countries such as Brazil, Russia, China, and India.

Expectations of "good" performance have escalated in the last hundred years. Back in 1900 the great German "Iron Chancellor" Bismarck demanded his investment adviser provide returns of 2% real. He was skeptical of even successful investment managers, reasoning that they would eventually be emasculated by getting either rich or old. As a result, he favored timberland, which in northern Europe had natural growth of about 2% per annum and which could be held forever. With timberland you didn't need professional investment management or have to worry about changing your asset allocation.

In my opinion, one of best investors in the world is David Swensen, who runs the Yale Endowment, and so I read the just released report of the endowment with great attention. He is a very clear and lucid thinker. As caveats, I disclose that I went to Yale and David is a very good friend of mine. However, his performance numbers verify my judgment of him even though his so-called "Yale Model" is currently being disparaged. As everyone knows, recent times have been very difficult for stocks and unusually good for bonds. The S&P 500 and almost every other index in the world are still well below the highs of 2000 and 2007. Bonds have beaten stocks, and asset classes such as private equity and opportunistic real estate have been crushed. Hedge funds also did not perform as advertised in the 2008 panic, although they fell far less than the popular indexes.

As one of the most revered heroes, Swensen has taken a lot of grief in the last couple of years as the Yale endowment declined from $22.8 billion to $16.6 billion. Bear in mind that the endowment provides about 40% of the operating budget of the university, so that over the last three years about $3 billion has been withdrawn but gifts were a partial offset. For the 20- and 10-year spans ending June 30, 2010, the endowment returned 13.1% per annum and 8.9%, respectively. A conventional portfolio invested 70% in stocks and 30% in bonds for the last 10 years returned 1.5% a year.

Swensen has always preached that the long-term investor should strive to be an owner rather than a lender. In the long run, the return to the owner of assets has to be higher than to the lender because the owner assumes more risk and volatility. In addition, the modern world has a bias towards inflation, which erodes, by definition, fixed-income returns. He views Treasury bonds as a liquidity reserve.

As noted above, equities have roundly beaten fixed income in modern times. However, the last decade has been a horrific one for equities, and so it is great tribute to his skills that he has done this well in one of the most difficult periods for "owners" in history. His other mantra is that "viewed in the time frame most appropriate for a long-term investor, well-chosen positions in illiquid assets perform better than otherwise comparable liquid assets." In other words, there is a liquidity premium embedded in publicly traded stocks. Yale was one the first big endowments or pension funds to invest heavily in private equity, venture capital, and hedge funds, and its asset allocation strategy that featured these illiquid asset categories and a miniscule allocation to bonds came to be known as the Yale Model.

For the last 10 years, as noted, Yale earned 8.9% per annum. Its private equity portfolio had a net return per annum of 6.2%, real estate 6.9%, absolute return (hedge funds) 11.1%, timber 12.1%, domestic equities 6.7%, oil and gas 24.7%, and foreign equities 13.8%. Over the same 10-year period, the S&P 500 returned minus 1.6% per annum. The numbers are interesting because in every case they exceed the median of the asset class, and also because Yale has a very elite, highly motivated group of people in their investment office. I'd like to know what venture capital and the small fixed-income portfolio returned. Even the best venture funds have made virtually nothing in the last decade.

So where is Yale now? Actually it's hard to really tell exactly because the only asset allocation we have is where they were on June 30, 2010, and where they were in the process of going at that time. However, here are some of the numbers versus the educational institution mean.

Asset Class	June 2010 Target (%)	June 2010 Actual (%)	Endowment Institution Mean (%)
Absolute Return	19.0	21.0	24.6
Domestic Equity	7.0	7.0	17.1
Fixed Income	4.0	4.0	15.3
Foreign Equity	9.0	9.9	18.1
Private Equity	33.0	30.3	10.2
Real Assets	28.0	27.5	11.6
Cash	0.0	0.4	2.8

As you can see, Yale is increasing its already huge allocation to private equity, which includes venture capital, with a target of 33% compared to 16% five years ago and 10% for the educational mean. I'm a little surprised. Swensen has a jaundiced eye in the best sense of the expression, and he has frequently expressed concerns about the leverage and even the concept of paying up to take a company private and then paying down to sell it. However, the text of the report says he expects to generate real returns of 10.5% with a risk of 27.7% from private equity. He also makes the point that there is huge dispersion in private equity firm returns, and that Yale with its tenure, staff, and analysis has a proven edge and entrée to investing with "the best." The dispersion between "the best" and the median is like 600 to 800 basis points.

I assume that David thinks that control, the ability to directly affect management, the judicious use of leverage, and alignment of interests are huge advantages for private equity firms. There is a theory going around that in public corporations, management's interests and the business process are not necessarily aligned with those of their stockholders and that they should thus sell at a discount to private companies. I think this is valid. However, I wonder how pure some of the private equity firms are.

Yale's increased allocation to private equity is being funded by a reduction in listed foreign and domestic equities from over 26% five years ago to just under 16% currently, with only 4% in U.S. stocks. I think big-cap, quality U.S. stocks are the cheapest, most liquid asset in the world. He probably thinks his managers can't add enough alpha to make them worthy. Yale believes in emerging markets with over half of its foreign equity portfolio targeted towards them and the report singles out China and India. It's also interesting that Yale, which pioneered hedge fund investing for institutions, is slightly reducing its allocation, which is actually down from 25% in 2008. I know he is very tough on fees and hurdle rates. Note the minuscule amount in fixed income, which defies the conventional wisdom.

In his introduction, Swensen summarizes his philosophy. "Viewed in the narrow time frame of crisis, liquid assets performed better than illiquid assets and safe assets performed better than risky assets. Viewed in a time frame more appropriate for a long-term investor, well-chosen positions in illiquid assets and well-selected portfolios of risky assets produce better returns than risk-free U.S. Treasury securities." This is the strategy that has put Yale at the top of the heap over the more than 20 years of Swensen's reign. There is no indication he is changing his mind. Reading the report suggests to me that Swensen does not believe the world is in for a double dip, a test of the 2009 lows, and a much longer secular bear market.

As for real assets, Yale has been big in real estate, oil and gas, and timberland for a number of years. The report cites "attractive return prospects, excellent portfolio diversification, and a hedge against unanticipated inflation." Again, discovering the most astute, honest managers is crucial, and hard work and constant monitoring is required. I don't see any allocation to farming and farmland, which I think is an attractive area, particularly outside the U.S.

In any case, the report is interesting reading, and it is available on the Yale Endowment web site.

In retrospect, the bears were right and I was too complacent. I was 90% net long with one good-sized short position in Brazil, which was a significant contributor to performance. As it turned out, I lost 1.7% for the month.

Meanwhile the global and U.S. economy have slowed fairly significantly in the last month or so, and it definitely seems the world is in another "soft patch." Real GDP forecasts have been significantly reduced for this year and in most cases for 2012. I don't think I need to go through all the specifics. The employment report today was another piece of evidence, as was ISI's latest weekly survey of China sales, which fell from 61.3 to 58.4.

The bears believe that at best this soft patch will last well into 2012 and at worst it will transition into the dreaded double dip with whiffs of deflation. They argue that the economic recovery never became self-sustaining, and that the financial crisis and deleveraging are not over. Furthermore, it is being compounded by a policy error as the U.S. eliminates fiscal stimulus and central banks elsewhere tighten monetary policy. The world is losing patience with the Europeans, who continue "to kick the Greece can down the road." Is the euro going to survive and what will be the unintended consequences? Meanwhile U.S. existing single-family home prices are still slowly but relentlessly sinking. The bear's conclusion: Stocks are going lower.

By contrast I believe this soft patch, particularly in the U.S., is temporary. Four of the principal causes of it are extraordinary and in all probability are going to reverse in the next few months. First, as oil prices rose, gasoline prices soared sapping consumer incomes everywhere. In the U.S., vehicle miles driven plunged, gas demand fell, and prices are now falling. Now with oil down $15 a barrel and threatening to go lower, the squeeze is gradually fading and spending numbers will improve.

Second, the weather ranging from floods to tornadoes has been horrific, particularly in the U.S. It has clearly had an effect on consumer and business activity. Assuming more normal weather, activity will improve and maybe even make up for the downturn.

Third, Japan is bouncing back. It is the third largest economy in the world and it was plunged into recession by the earthquake and tsunami. Japanese production and exports fell 15% in March. The Japanese mobilized and repaired their broken factories, mended the roads, and have gotten their economy going again. The Japanese production PMI rose above 50 in May. Toyota, Hitachi, and Sony are just a few of the manufacturing companies that have got their factories back on line faster than expected and in some cases are running at 100% capacity, even on weekends.

Fourth, a related Japan effect is the global disruption of supply chains as Japanese plants that produced specialized components were shut down for repairs. There is no question that companies around the world have suffered as a result and summer shutdowns were moved up. As production fell, auto inventories in the U.S. reached the lowest level in years and this affected vehicle sales in May. Ward's is saying production will increase dramatically in June and July, which is great news for the economy.

The global economy may fade after the bounce or it may not. If Europe surprised by moving towards fiscal integration to combine with its monetary integration, that would be very important for confidence. In the U.S. everyone including me thinks house prices are going lower, but with prices falling, family incomes improving, and mortgage rates down, affordability is at a record high by a large amount.

Bounce coming in both economies and stocks is my guess.

The "Atlantic Crisis"

In mid-June I went on a trip to Asia. First stop was Korea, then Hong Kong, Indonesia, and finally Singapore. As always, there is nothing like getting out of NYC and being on the ground talking to real people. Thanks to my friend James Cheng, the brilliant head of Morgan Stanley Investment Management Asia, we had particularly stimulating meetings in Hong Kong and China. For example, out of Hong Kong, James arranged a cruise of successful young entrepreneur Michael Lee Tze Hau's yacht up into the islands with a half-dozen Hong Kong and Chinese private equity guys and their girlfriends. Six hours with this bunch was worth more than 10 three-day bank conferences and all the economists' blather. They were the essence of Silicon Valley mentality, which is what breeds innovation, creative destruction, and dynamic growth. Here is what I wrote at the time.

■ ■ ■

June 21, 2011

They are calling it the "Atlantic Crisis" in Asia; 1998 was the "Asian Crisis" when the Asians themselves were the principal perpetrators. This one is potentially much bigger and made in the USA and Europe. It took years for the Asians to pick up the pieces and for equities to recover. Our rehab may be longer and more painful, but they mostly think their economies and markets are going to be fine, even bubbly, as ours were in the late 1990s and 2006–2007. I agree with them.

Here I am in Indonesia being bitten by real and financial no-see-ums and licking my wounds from the last couple of weeks. I pulled back a little by selling short some more of a luxury goods basket, but basically I have given back most of my gains for the year to date. Very painful! However, I still believe that we are on the verge of a bounce in the U.S.,

Asian, and Japanese economies, and that the Germans, the ECB, and the Europeans are not so crazy and stupid they will commit Hara-Kiri. What bothers me is whether kicking the can down the road again is just another form of disembowelment. Spain is the monster that terrifies me.

Meanwhile, the global inventory correction is not yet complete but there are encouraging signs from Japan, U.S. auto production, capital spending surveys, and ECRI. Unfortunately the U.S. political establishment still does not have its act together although there are encouraging rumors of two mammoth deals.

I have been in Asia 10 days now and have been in Korea, Hong Kong, China, and now Indonesia. I have talked with a lot of businessmen, entrepreneurs, and investors. You have to hear them and see for yourself to understand the dynamism and the creative destruction that is going on. The entrepreneur who two years ago hustled an order from Drada to manufacture shoes. Bought an old building in Shenzhen. Made good money, but now Drada (fictional name) is canceling orders on him. Fancy shoe sales America and Europe anemic. He shrugs.

"I'm going to cut and run," he tells me. "Lay off 2,000 girls. Shut the old joint down. But you know what? I've got sweet music playing in the interior. Four retail stores with same store sales running up 30 to 40%." This in essence is the bull China story. Transition from export, infrastructure capital goods–driven growth to domestic demand. My bet is it works with soft landing, 6–7% three-year growth trend for the second biggest economy in the world and 4–5% inflation, which sums to 10–12% nominal. Quant studies show low correlation intermediate equity market performance and real GDP but strong with nominal.

We went to see Huawei, the Chinese telecommunications equipment manufacturer and tormentor of Cisco and Ericsson. What a story! Privately owned by its 150,000 employees. Revenues about $25 billion. Spends 6% on R&D versus 13% for Ericsson and has higher margins. Reason they say is scientists and engineers cost so much less in China but are hungrier and more productive. Their researchers are formed into teams, operate separately, and compete fiercely with each other. The big U.S. and European tech companies have cooperative but bureaucratic development programs.

Huawei's founder was and is a Chinese version of Steve Jobs with a communist social bent. A former army engineer, he owns 1.5%. Last week the company announced a 7-inch tablet computer running Android, with a 10-incher on the way. The new line is called the Media Pad and it will come with a dual-core 1.2 GHz processor from Qualcomm and with applications like Facebook and Twitter. But what do I know about tech? Absolutely nothing.

In fact, for that matter, what does anyone know about China, bulls and bears alike? The answer is "nobody knows nuthin"! All the pontification and statistics are total BS. You either believe or you don't. I believe.

Some Sunday night this summer, China will announce one more tightening but will say it's the last one. Leadership fears inflation but dreads a hard landing and unemployment even more. Chinese markets will soar. Tough issue is how to own them. H-Share Index dominated by financials when you want to own mid-cap domestic demand–driven companies.

Turn Off Your Bloomberg and Tune Out the Babel

Here is what I wrote four days before my hip operation, and here is the chart of what the S&P 500 looked like. I now attach the title "Creepy Creeping." I was still about 90% net long. The biggest contributor for the month of June was my holdings in Japan and particularly a China-focused Japan basket. I should have paid more attention to the weakness of my "Old U.S. Technology" basket and China and Hong Kong. I also had put a short on a basket we had built of "Global Luxury Retailers," which went against me.

■ ■ ■

July 7, 2011

Well, we are back to where we were about a month ago, and I picked up a few bruises on the bumpy roller-coaster ride. I did nothing brilliant in June but at least didn't get stopped out at the bottom as I'm afraid so many did. In fact I barely traded at all. I

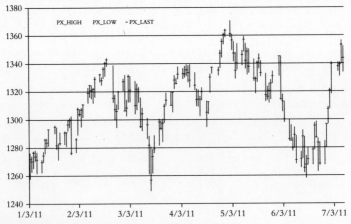

Creepy Creeping: S&P 500 1/3/11–7/8/11

Data source: Bloomberg

suspect the use of tight stop-loss limits is going to turn out to be the bane of the proprietary trading cult. A lot of P&L and head damage has been inflicted in the last week. As always, the barn doors are slammed after the horses have run and the victims vow in unison "never again." The stop-loss mania is similar to the French building and relying on the Maginot Line in the 1930s.

The Economist this week has a good essay about "information overload" and the data fog from the onslaught of e-mails. It cites studies that show it creates anxiety, a feeling of powerlessness, reduces creativity, and makes people less productive. The solution: Filter information and from time to time turn off your phone and the Internet, and reflect in peace and quiet. I'm convinced that prop traders focused on short-term market momentum, stops, and the high-frequency data are becoming victims of this mindless volatility and are burning themselves and their performance out. They deride "investors" as "dinosaurs." And I know it's a different business model, but I think we want to be "investors" and have a medium-term view that we stick to until the facts change. My view is that the most likely case is that the most likely medium-term outlook is that the global economy improves over the summer, cans do get kicked down the road, and that with stocks the cheapest asset class—in other words, the best house in a bad neighborhood—they move higher. I suggest turning off your Bloomberg and tuning out of the e-mail babble from the likes of me.

Last week, the Europeans kicked the can down the road to perdition again, buying some time and opportunity, but it remains to be seen whether Greece (or for that matter the other beleaguered European countries) can deliver some austerity. Fundamentally, Greece is a totally structurally dysfunctional economy. What were the Europeans thinking about when they let Greece into the euro block? Eventually, Washington over the next few weeks will boot its budget can far into the future but it will be lip service to entitlements. Meanwhile, the economic bounce we've been looking for in the U.S., Japan, and Asia seems to be forthcoming as industrial production in the U.S., Japan, and Asia is rebounding. The issue is now what for equity markets? Was last week just an oversold, short-covering rally or the beginning of something worthwhile? My inclination is that the most likely case is that equity markets are going higher, maybe by as much as another 10–15%.

The high-frequency data over the summer are bound to be mixed and volatile, as the global inventory adjustment is not yet complete and will dampen global manufacturing. Japan is in a V-shaped recovery from the earthquake demand and supply shock, but Europe is struggling, and the ECB's raising rates is not helpful. Consumer spending, confidence, capital investment, and employment must improve to support a second leg in the global economy and markets, and I think it will. As food and energy prices fall, disposable income growth and spending should pick up in Asia, North and South America, and maybe even in Europe. In the U.S., stronger consumer spending in the third quarter should boost sales, and with companies having resisted rehiring, productivity gains could boost margins by about two percentage points in the next year.

As for the second biggest economy in the world, China, the PMI, USDA June data, and the 100-city property index all provide evidence China has slowed and inflation has peaked. As I've said before, "nobody knows nuthin'" about China, but when the Prime Minister Wen Jiabao, on a high-profile tour of Europe, said last week inflation in China is under control, you can bet the official statistics in the next few months are going to show it's under control. It's fashionable to be negative and bad-mouth China, but I think the bears are wrong. I continue to believe Chinese shares, H shares, MSCI China, and Hong Kong (luxury property) are going to be winners here and now. Japanese stocks are going higher, too, and I own the big-cap exporters.

In the U.S. in the midst of all the gloom in June, analysts' top-down estimates of earnings for 2011 fell only marginally to $94.87 for operating earnings and $94.23 for reported. For 2012, the numbers are $99 and $97.50 respectively. Not bad! Macro analysts are bound to be very affected by the overall atmosphere, and these minor reductions show the resilience of corporate earnings power. Investor sentiment collapsed and the hedge fund net long fell prior to last week but will probably snap back now. It will be very bullish if it doesn't. ISI estimates Q2 S&P profits will be up 16%, beating forecasts by 2%.

I'm still an owner of U.S. technology, oil services, and industrial machinery shares. The rise and fall of RIMM is sobering. Is the market right in valuing Apple as vulnerable, too? I'm inclined to believe Apple is a very cheap, big-cap growth stock and that it ought to have a few more big products and at least one more major price move in it. I'm thinking my basket of consumer luxury goods short is a good hedge. The stocks are so expensive they will lag the more cyclical sectors if the markets keep rallying, and if, God forbid, the indexes falter, they will sink like stones. Why should Apple sell at 12 times the next 12 months' earnings when consumer fads cruise along at 30 to 50 times?

The New Face of China

July 11, 2011

O n my visit to China last month, we went to Huawei, which is a huge Chinese telecommunications, network, and technology company that you can think of as the Chinese version of Cisco. What is so fascinating about Huawei is that it may be the formidable face, the model, of the New Chinese company. My guide was my friend James Cheng, who runs Asia for Morgan Stanley Investment Management. James is a very erudite, wise man who studies China and Chinese companies intensely. Huawei is very impressive, and since there is no public market for its shares, it has no shareholder relations people. James arranged for us to have a long lunch session with a senior executive and a translator. The guy was inscrutable, clearly a strategic thinker, and answered our questions directly but didn't volunteer anything. He did say business was still good despite the global soft patch, and that revenues and earnings were in line for gains comparable to the year before.

The company does publish an annual report in English full of pretty pictures, which must have been written by a public relations firm. It is long and not very informative. The company wants you to know it "Thinks Green" and is women-friendly. It does disclose that last year Huawei got two thirds of its revenues from outside of China and a third from China. Its business was two thirds telecom networks with the other 33% from global services and devices, whatever that means.

In the early spring of 2000 in Boston, I attended a Cisco presentation that was stunning. At the time the company had the biggest market cap in the world. John Chambers in all his articulate glory laid out the future, and his lieutenants, bright-eyed and bushy-tailed, elaborated with groomed presentations. What they and I didn't know was that there was a Chinese tiger lying out there waiting for them that was going to be very

Huawei Vital Statistics

(USD Billion)	2010		2009		2008	
	Ericsson	Huawei	Ericsson	Huawei	Ericsson	Huawei
Fx Rate/USD	0.139	0.147	0.139	0.146	0.139	0.146
Revenue	28.3	27.2	28.6	21.8	29.1	18.3
COGS	17.9	15.8	18.9	13.1	18.7	11.0
COGS % Sales	63%	58%	66%	60%	64%	60%
SG&A	3.8	4.6	3.7	3.5	3.7	3.3
SG&A % of Sales	13%	17%	13%	16%	13%	18%
Total SG&A +COGS	77%	75%	79%	76%	77%	78%
Operating Margin	8%	16%	3%	14%	8%	13%
Net Profit	1.6	3.5	0.6	2.7	1.6	1.1
Net Profit Margin	6%	13%	2%	12%	6%	6%
R&D	4.4	2.4	4.6	1.9	4.7	1.5
R&D % of Sales	16%	9%	16%	9%	16%	8%
R&D Staff	20,000	51,000	18,300	43,600	19,800	37,626
R&D/Staff	220,000	47,647	251,366	43,578	237,374	39,866

Wages	6.0	3.7	5.7	3.1	5.4	N/A
Social Security	1.9	0.8	1.9	0.5	1.8	N/A
Total	7.9	4.5	7.6	3.6	7.2	N/A
Total Employee	90,261	111,000	82,493	95,000	78,740	87,502
Total Wage/Employee	88,061	40,586	92,129	38,074	91,440	N/A
Revenue/Employee	313,535	245,045	346,696	229,474	369,571	209,138
Total Asset	39.2	23.6	37.5	20.4	39.7	N/A
Goodwill/Intangibles	6.4	0.1	6.7	0.1	N/A	N/A
Total Equity	20.4	8.1	19.6	6.3	19.6	N/A

Source: Huawei Annual Report and other documents

price competitive. In the decade since, Huawei has deeply wounded the other telecom network and communications companies. James calculates that the five biggest have lost over 75% of their market value since then. Basically Huawei has sucked the growth momentum out of both them and presumably their cohorts and suppliers. Huawei's revenues over the last five years have compounded annually at 29% a year in RMBs, operating profit at 57%, and total cash flow from operations at 49%. This analysis was prepared by James.

What stands out is that Huawei spends 9% of sales on R&D compared to 16% for Ericsson and about the same for Cisco, yet it has far more employees in research and pays them a lot less. The reason, the guy we were with said, is that they can hire the best Chinese engineers at much lower wages and social security costs than can the Western companies. These people are motivated by the environment at Huawei and also by the stock ownership. When you read the bios of the Supervisory Board of Huawei, the people who actually run the company, they all went to Chinese technical universities and there is no evidence of U.S. training.

The president and founder of the company is Ren Zhengfei. He was born in 1944 into a rural family in a remote mountain town in Guizhou province. Both his parents were schoolteachers. He somehow got into and graduated from an engineering college, and then worked in civil engineering until 1974 when he joined the elite army engineering corps. He was noticed, and was invited to attend the National Science conference four years later and then the 12th annual conference of the Communist Party in 1982. In 1983 as policy changed the government disbanded the engineering corps, and he retired from the army. He worked for the next four years in engineering and logistics for the Shenzhen South Sea Oil Company. "Dissatisfied," his bio says, he started Huawei in 1987 with capital of 21,000RMB. He still runs the company. This is the sparse, official biography of a great 67-year-old entrepreneur. He must have had an amazing journey.

Huawei is not "publicly owned" in our sense of the word. Its shares are held by 65,000 of its 110,000 employees, and they elect the board of directors and supervisory board. The largest single shareholder is Ren Zhengfei himself, who owns about 1.5% of the outstanding stock, our lunch companion told us. The chairman is a woman, Sun Yafang. It is not clear when an employee begins to be awarded stock, but he or she gets it at book value at the time of acquisition and presumably gets more or has some taken away from time to time. When the employee leaves or retires he or she sells the holding back to the company at the current book value. Book value has been compounding at 40% a year.

This system was the wealth-creating, people-attracting model that the U.S. investment banks formerly had before they went public and crazy. It made me rich at Morgan Stanley. It's a great model. Employees that own book value stock are much less inclined to do stupid, risky, short-term things. Corporate headquarters, marketing, much of R&D, and some manufacturing are in a huge company town within the giant city of Shenzhen across the bridge from Hong Kong. The Huawei facility is very attractive, with schools, restaurants, retail stores, and sports facilities integrated. All this is a far cry from the sweatshop facilities we saw elsewhere or where you read young, depressed girls are jumping out of windows.

Of course investment banks are trying to persuade Huawei to go public. "We like our system the way it is," the guy at lunch said. "It helps us to attract the best talent." He did say the company's Middle East business is growing rapidly. Two weeks ago Huawei announced a line of "mobile broadband converged home devices," new optical transmission equipment, and optical access and core networks. After lunch we saw demonstrations of these and other products. I understood nothing.

The bear story on Huawei is as follows. The Chinese army really owns and runs the company, they say. Some years ago the sneaky Chinese bought Cisco equipment, copied it, and as proof that it was copied, the instruction manuals have the same typos as the original Cisco manuals. They are R&D sterile and have no capacity to develop commercial new products. The model is fatally flawed. We asked the guy at lunch about all this. The translator winced, but the executive just shook his head and "thinly" smiled. Looks like sour grapes to me.

My friend James Cheng says Huawei is not the typical big Chinese company, but he has about 50 or 60 other companies that are using this model successfully. It's something to think deeply about. As more Chinese companies use this model, they can create their own Silicon Valley, Googles, and Facebooks.

Back home every involved investor should read David Brooks in yesterday's *New York Times*. Brooks is the most respected conservative Republican, and his views have force. Brooks writes that the Gang of Six and the Democrats have offered major changes in Social Security, Medicare, and tax policy by lowering the base rate and broadening the base. The result is a total package that would reduce the deficit

by $4 trillion, and the size of the federal government by a historic rela-
tive amount over 10 years. Obama's concessions could fracture the liberal
base of the Democratic Party, Brooks writes. It's "an historic opportunity" for his party, he says, and he is baffled and disgusted the Hard Right
is so adamant in the face of the precipice. Obama may end up as the
winner even if we go over the cliff as people catch on.

The Senate seems to understand this, but the House and the Tea Party
are still resisting. If the U.S. defaults, Tuesday's rally is classic Fools' Gold.
With at least an economic bounce coming and a huge shot of confidence from a deal, the S&P could surge 15 pc. If no compromise, down
10 pc. Note the massive liquidity and the Bloomberg story today about
Soros and Moore Capital being on the sidelines. You can bet almost every
major pension fund is underweight stocks.

Europe is still the same old mess. I think the best macro play on a
U.S. happy ending is China FXI Hong Kong, H shares, all of which I
own. Since summer 2009 China has underperformed emerging market
index by 35 pc and EM has lagged developed markets for last six months.
Earnings up 20 pc last year, probably a little less this year. Multiples low
teens. I don't believe the China bears. My net is long about 70 pc, very
risky ledge considering irrationality of U.S. politicians, and that includes
20 pc S&P short. More signs of a deal and I go 90 pc net long.

Harvesting the "Grapes of Our Own Wrath"

Here I am in the midst of rehab moaning and groaning about the market.
It was a sour time for everyone, not just me.

■ ■ ■

August 3, 2011

It's August 3rd and it's a sour and agonizingly difficult time. I've been doing this for almost 40 years, and I can't recall as tough an environment. There were plenty of terrifying moments of panic and crisis in the past, but at least they were analyzable and you could assess the risks in making your bets. This time I'm losing faith in the ability of America and Europe to make and implement the very hard but absolutely necessary decisions we are faced with. We are truly harvesting the grapes of our own wrath.

I've been too optimistic about America's politicians eventually doing the right thing and also about the health of the economy. The U.S. inevitably must reduce entitlements and defense spending and raise tax rates on the rich. I'm a long-time supply-sider, but we have become an unfair, unbalanced society. It's just plain wrong that GE doesn't pay any taxes. It's not fair that hedge fund and private equity guys get a tax break on their carried interest earnings. The tax code has been distorted by the lobbyists. President Obama at one point proposed raising the Social Security retirement and Medicare ages but then scurried for cover when the screams sounded. In the final debates and sound bites, everyone, Democrat, Republican, or Tea Party, pledged that Social Security would not be touched. Has America become ungovernable? Is the two-year term for Congress an anachronism of colonial times?

Unfortunately Europe's leaders are no better. The first rule of central banking as ordained by Walter Baghot is that in a crisis and a panic, the Authorities must always risk doing too much—overkill—rather than doing too little because the price of having to save the system a second time with bigger bailouts will be immeasurably, perhaps catastrophically, higher. I'm afraid that's what just happened. Spreads are widening.

Japan since 1990 is an example of the ravages of political failure. A large but localized speculative bubble was allowed to metastasize into 20 years of stag-deflation. The LDP's one-party government of tired old men was structurally unable to make the financial and market reforms that were required, and 20 years of stag-deflation were the result. In the late 1930s, bad reads and mistakes prolonged the Great Recession that finally was only cured by World War II. I'm wondering if we are stumbling into the same quagmire. Thirty years of economic policy of avoiding recessions at all costs has resulted in a crisis when both fiscal and monetary policy are impotent. Interest rates in the U.S. are zero, and the deficit is 10% of GDP.

Further complicating the picture is the evidence that the U.S. recession was deeper and the recovery was weaker than the statistics indicated. Now the high-frequency data are indicating that the economy is weakening again. There are those who still maintain we are going to get a bounce in the next few months, but I am afraid they are grasping for straws. Europe also is soft. Italian automobile sales fell 14% month over month in July, the Brazil PMI dropped, and in confirmation the global manufacturing PMI declined from 52.3 to 50.6. Both businessmen and consumers are appalled and disconcerted and are sensibly sitting on their hands. Unemployment will probably be going up rather than down.

Will the Fed act? Probably. But unlike last summer, I doubt whether a QE3 announcement will be a jolt of confidence that will revive the stock market much less the economy. Perhaps a new program to buy existing single-family homes or mortgages might work. House prices do seem to have stabilized, and as the biggest repository of wealth, a sustained 10% up-tick would do a lot for consumer confidence and spending.

So what to do now? I'm 50% net long with short hedges on in the S&P 500, Germany, Brazil, and luxury brands. I'm still long big-cap tech, oil service, and big-capitalization quality-growth stocks in the U.S. I also remain very committed to Asia, ranging from the China complex to Korea, Thailand, and Indonesia. I also own Japan. As I have described previously, I continue to believe this is an American-European crisis, not an Asian crisis.

I'm also convinced that the cheapest big-liquid currency in the world is the dollar. Purchasing power parity, which is another version of reversion to the mean, is my religion. Speaking with Europeans this summer, I am struck by how cheap they think New York City is, from hotels and restaurants to apartments, and believe it or not Europeans are finding Fairfield County real estate very attractive.

The Economist this week has a fascinating piece on their Big Mac Index. They have now refined their calculations to take into account the "Balassa-Samuelson effect" of wages and average prices, always cheaper in poorer countries. Purchasing power parity and their old index signaled where exchange rates should be headed in the long run but said little about today's equilibrium rate. However, the relationship between prices and GDP per person (income per head, in other words) can perhaps be better used to estimate the current fair value of the currencies.

Their calculations show the euro is 36% overvalued versus the dollar, and the Brazilian real is around 100%, adjusting for this sensible refinement. Sweden and Switzerland also have expensive currencies, which should be no surprise to anyone who has paid a hotel bill there recently. The exchange rates in Italy, Portugal, Spain, and Greece are all overvalued versus Germany, which of course is part of the European problem. By contrast, contrary to the conventional wisdom, the RMB is not undervalued and the yen is not particularly inflated. Some emerging market currencies are still undervalued versus the dollar.

So what does this say? The big anomaly in the world is the dollar, particularly if you are a European, a Swede, a Swiss, a Brazilian, or, surprisingly, an Argentinean. Own and buy dollar-denominated assets! Quality U.S. stocks are dollar-denominated pieces of paper with a call on earning assets around the world and an income stream in dollars. As this is written, the U.S. market now is down eight days in a row, and some of our sentiment measures are flashing. The Wilmot Risk Appetite Index has dropped into panic territory for the first time since March 2009. I'm getting tempted. A few more days of this, and we are going to get a powerful rally.

No More Water, the Fire Next Time

About a week later I wrote this lament.

■ ■ ■

This is a selling panic of incredible, mind-numbing ferocity. No one can predict outcomes, but my guess is we must be only a day or two away from a powerful rally that could retrace half of the decline of the last two weeks. History suggests that a scary retest of the lows will follow. All my contrarian instincts are aroused by the intense fear and enormous oversold condition of the markets. You want to buy fear and big dips. There is plenty of both around currently.

However, having had my fingers badly burned covering a major short in the DAX index a few days and 7% ago, I'm not ready to commit capital until there is some stability or good news. I'm totally convinced this has to be a very bad, wrong time to buy gold and sell stocks, but as a fiduciary I've got to protect capital. I do not want to get down more than 5% for the year. I don't think it's in any way similar, but the last two weeks are reminiscent of the fall of 2008 and Lehman. I want to see some decent high-frequency economic numbers for the U.S. to diminish odds of a double dip. I also want to see signs of a solution to the sovereign debt crisis in Europe. Neither is happening yet. But when I see those, I will load up! Stocks are incredibly cheap.

However, I do think the extent and magnitude of this decline is going to get the attention of the politicians in America and Europe. The markets are disgusted. We Bidn't know it, but the markets watched the charade and having read the Bible, whispered ". . . then God gave Noah the Rainbow Sign. No more water, the fire next time." Talk, hollow promises of budget cuts in the future, inadequate bond-buying programs

128

in Europe won't work, and the markets have lost patience. In the U.S. some politician has to stand up on his or her hind legs and tell the country unequivocally we've got to extend the retirement age for Social Security to 70, we've got to change the rules on Medicare, we've got to reform the tax code and raise tax rates on the rich. And we have to cut the defense budget huge. As for Europe, the final step has to be the fiscal integration of Euroland. I don't know about Europeans, but Americans are ready to hear the truth. "Ye shall know the truth and the truth shall set you free."

On the other hand, this frightening collapse, particularly so soon after 2008, will scar the psyche of the investor class. I believe it will intensify the skepticism about hedge funds and high investment management fees. I doubt the U.S. is going to "double dip," but the longer this chaos goes on, the greater the effect on consumer and business confidence. Remember, though, that corporate balance sheets are very strong, earnings are still healthy, and the Asian economies are expanding. The economy shrugged off the Crash of 1987 and the bubble-burst of 2000–2002. I still believe in U.S. tech, oil service, the global multinationals, and Asia.

The Valley of Death

August 15, 2011

*H*ere we go again, "half a league, half a league onward" into the Valley of Death that is the August 2011 stock markets. The last couple of weeks from time to time I've felt as though I were caught in "The Charge of the Light Brigade" in Tennyson's wonderful poem. I'll give you just two stanzas for titillation.

Cannon to the right of them,
Cannon to the left of them
Cannon in front of them
   Volley'd and thunder'd;
Storm'd at by shot and shell,
Boldly they rode and well,
Into the jaws of Death,
Into the mouth of Hell
   Rode the six hundred.

Flash'd all their sabers bare,
Flash'd as they turned in air
Sabring the gunners there.
Charging an army while
   All the world wonder'd.
Plunged in the battery-smoke
Right thro' the line they broke;
Cossack and Russian
Reel'd from the sabre-stroke
   Shatter'd and sunder'd.
Then they rode back, but not
   Not the six-hundred.

The troopers in that historic charge "knew someone had blundered" but "theirs not to make reply; theirs but to do and die." However, we are different and I'm outraged to learn from Bloomberg that 75% of the volume so far this month has been from high-frequency trading (HFT). My beloved stock market, the citadel of free market capitalism, and a key barometer of business and consumer confidence, has been over-run, violated, raped by HFT. I don't believe I know any HFT people, much less how their algorithms work, but as I understand it, as explained by Bloomberg, HFT is a technique that relies on the rapid and automated placement of orders, many of which are immediately updated or canceled, as part of strategies such as market making and statistical arbitrage and tactics based on momentum, taking a position, and entering multiple, supporting orders that are then canceled.

Wonderful! Great! The irrational violence we are being tortured by is being propelled and consciously created by algorithms driven by raw momentum, and which try to create price intimidation and volatility. Mindless volatility, which is the friend and companion of HFT, but which also raises the risk premium. In many ways HFT is similar to the Program Trading mania, which resulted in the Crash of 1987. It turned out that the violence of that October had no discernible effect on the economy but did result in a significant withdrawal from equities, which took several years to reverse.

So how do you invest now? I'm a cowardly bull. I think high-quality equities have discounted a mild recession and an earnings decline of 10–15%, are deeply oversold, and are the best place to be in a world plagued by incompetence in the U.S. and Europe. I don't think a double-dip recession is the most likely outcome, and I do believe in what George Will calls "American exceptionalism." We will overcome this partisan, political malaise. China and Brazil have the resources and will keep growing. The emerging markets, particularly the Asian ones, are growth engines. Capitalist economies will not just endure, they will prevail. Equities are the place to be for the long run. But this ride through the Valley of Death and the atrocity that HFT is aiding and abetting could be very bad for the perception of equities.

The other issue is that the U.S. market is very sensitive to what happens in Europe in regard to the sovereign debt issue, and no resolution seems to be forthcoming. The much heralded Merkel-Sarkozy meeting today was a dud. Meanwhile the Euroland economy is even more languid than ours.

I also am plagued by the fear that although equities now look cheap based on the past 25 years, based on pre-1980 valuations they are not.

This is a long and complicated subject, but the data show that from 1849 through 2010 the real (inflation-adjusted) return from equities in the U.S. has been 6.2% per annum, which is very satisfactory.

Here is the way I break the history down. Incidentally the real growth in corporate profits has only been 2% per annum over this period.

1857–1881   Secular bull market following Civil War, opening of West, annual real return 11.1%

1882–1894   Sluggish aftermath with annual real return 2.9%

1895–1908   Industrial development, inventions, foreign expansion, reflation, annual real return 9.8%

1909–1922   13 years, growth slows, inflation, World War I, problems, bust of 1920, annual return minus 2.5%

1922–1930   Boom and huge speculative bubble, annual return 22.4%

1930–1946   16 years of bust, depression, World War II minus 1.3% annually age of bonds

1947–1966   Long secular bull, bonds fade, McChesney Martin Fed, annual real return 8.3%

1967–1981   14 years vicious stagflation-driven bear market 2.8%, real return 2.8%

1982–1999   Disinflation, secular bull market in stocks and bonds, 13.6% annually in equities

1999–?   Bubble bursts and aftermath with two secular bear markets so far

The disconcerting thought when perusing this history is that Professor Rogoff is right. History shows that after bubbles the aftermaths are prolonged and the average over the last century and a half is just under 14 years. It could be said we are 11 into this one.

So where do I come out? If investing were just all history, the historians would be billionaires. Same with quants and algorithms. High-quality stocks in the U.S. and the emerging markets are the place to be, and this panic is a wonderful opportunity to buy them. We will limit our year-to-date drawdown to mid-single-digit levels and stand ready to further cut our exposure as we approach that level. Cowardly, but my family's money is in the fund as well. So I'm keeping my net long at about 60%, waiting for the fog of war to clear some, and counting on being quick enough to hitch a ride if the beast rallies.

Lest We Forget

Recovering from a hip replacement operation and in rehab I am not in the best of spirits. Once again I resort to poetry. Close friends running hedge funds were telling me of their market-inflicted afflictions, which ranged from insomnia to diarrhea. I actually made money in July but lost 4% in August.

■ ■ ■

August 30, 2011

We are not likely to soon forget the fear of those weeks in August when the HFT ruled the world. The ebb and flow of the battle for investment survival have been sleep depriving and agonizing because there is always a chance that our system is so fragile that it will careen over the cliff and we must always remember that the battle is about enhancing the purchasing power of capital but also about survival of your and our money.

The investment situation today is both perilous and rife with opportunities. On one side looms the abyss of bungling incompetence, a double dip, and a frightening fall back to the lows; on the other, "broad, sun-lit uplands." In *East of Eden*, John Steinbeck's great saga of the 1930s dust bowl and the Aggies, a recurring, powerful message it preaches is that "it never failed that during the dry years the people forgot the rich years and during the wet years they lost all memory of the dry years." We as investors have to be careful not to fall into the same trap, and it might not be a tender one because a violent move up to equilibrium valuations is not inconceivable. We have lived through an equities dust bowl of our own that has already lasted 12 years and counting.

There is still a lot of gloom and doom out there, but the messages from Bernanke and Christine Lagarde last week at Jackson Hole were concise and to the point. We, the West, and our politicians have to get our act together. Our economies desperately need stimulus and employment.

But we must also impose long-term fiscal discipline on our bloated entitlement structures. There seems to be a consensus developing that the underwater mortgage issue has to be dealt with.

The U.S. has to raise the Social Security retirement age five, not two, years. Medicare has to be reformed. The size of government has to be pared. The defense budget has to be ruthlessly cut from 5% of GDP to 2% like everyone else. It's utterly ridiculous that we are spending as much on defense as the rest of the world combined and that the Office of the President's staff has tripled in the last 15 years. Who do we, America, think we are that we are exempt from the laws of excess, hubris, and deficits?

In 1897, as England, at the height of the power and glory of the British empire, celebrated the Golden Jubilee of the reign of Queen Victoria with an opulent party that marked the absolute peak of the British empire, Rudyard Kipling, the poet laureate of arms and soldiering, alarmed by the hubris and the waste, wrote this poem, which he titled "Recessional." Our issues today are different, but it echoes across the years. Are we becoming one with Nineveh and Tyre? Lest we forget the regime that made us great, "Far-called our navies melt away."

> God of our fathers, known of old —
> Lord of our far-flung battle line —
> Beneath whose awful hand we hold
> Dominion over palm and pine —
> Lord God of Hosts, be with us yet,
> Lest we forget—lest we forget!
>
> The tumult and the shouting dies —
> The Captains and the Kings depart —
> Still stands Thine ancient sacrifice,
> An humble and a contrite heart.
> Lord God of Hosts, be with us yet,
> Lest we forget—lest we forget!
>
> Far-called our navies melt away —
> On dune and headland sinks the fire —
> Lo, all our pomp of yesterday
> Is one with Nineveh and Tyre!
> Judge of the Nations, spare us yet,
> Lest we forget—lest we forget!

If, drunk with sight of power, we loose
Wild tongues that have not Thee in awe —
Such boastings as the Gentiles use,
Or lesser breeds without the Law —
Lord God of Hosts, be with us yet,
Lest we forget—lest we forget!

For heathen heart that puts her trust
In reeking tube and iron shard —
All valiant dust that builds on dust,
And guarding calls not Thee to guard.
For frantic boast and foolish word,
Thy Mercy on Thy People, Lord!
Amen.

Being an optimist, I don't think we will forget and that our form of governance will not just endure but will prevail. However, for equity markets to keep moving higher from here, the West must deal with its issues. I'm 70+% net long, with the U.S. and Asia still the principal focus. I have covered the short in the luxury goods basket and added to China, technology, and U.S. industrial equipment companies (Deere, Caterpillar, United Technologies, etc.).

"If You're Going through Hell, Keep Going!"

Winston S. Churchill said, "If You're Going through Hell, Keep Going!" During the dark days of World War II when England stood alone, Churchill always preached perseverance and as a congenital optimist that there were always "broad sunlit uplands" on the other side. Well, we, tortured by volatility, certainly are going through an economic and market hell, and what makes it so difficult is that on one side of this hell looms the apocalypse, and on the other, a bull move in stocks. It will be a career-threatening event to get it wrong. Nevertheless, we have to keep going, but nothing has happened in the last two weeks to engender confidence. Europe is that tail that is wagging the U.S. market.

The apocalypse case is a double-dip recession and a decline in equities from here of 20% or so back towards the lows of 2009. Neither the Authorities in Europe nor the U.S. can get their acts together, and both continents are discontentedly drifting into unhappy versions of the last 20 years in Japan. In other words, decades of ineffective leadership, mild deflation, economic stagnation, and a prolonged, perhaps 10-year, secular, not cyclical, bear market. As the stagnation unfolds, the emerging markets will also languish, and China will probably unravel as its debt bubble explodes. If you want to get really bearish on China, read *Red Capitalism* (John Wiley & Sons, 2011) by Carl E. Walter and Fraser J.T. Howie.

The more restrained bears say the apocalypse will be "Japan Light," but the deep bears argue it could be "Japan Heavy." The difference between light and heavy versions derives from the argument that Japan is a country with a homogeneous society without the racial and income discrepancies of the U.S. and Europe. The Japanese are a relatively tranquil people that docilely accept pain and the status quo, and who are not inclined to taking to the streets and lynch mobs. Nevertheless their stock market is still down 60% from its highs of 22 years ago. By contrast the

Americans and Europeans are much less likely to be either patient or tolerant of a comatose economy, wealth destruction, and political mumbling. After all, the Great Depression spawned guys named Hitler and Stalin, National Socialism, and Communism.

We have been through hell but I fear we have not yet got through hell. As I have referenced before, the convulsive poem of the bears is William Butler Yeats's great classic, "The Second Coming," written in the dark depths of the 1920s. This is a deeply, profoundly bearish poem with some rather obscure references. In the first stanza the expanding spiral of the falcon's flight symbolizes the ominously spiraling course of history. Once again the lines "the best lack all conviction and the worst are full of passionate intensity" resonate. In the second stanza the sphinxlike creature, a beast, with "a gaze blank and pitiless as the sun" is suggestive of evil, and for the poet, symbolic of the period of history about to begin. The "beast" was present at the First Coming, presumably the birth of Christ, but was helpless before what Yeats calls the "uncontrollable mystery" of the birth of the Son of God. However, the Second Coming is an entirely another matter.

> Turning and turning in the widening gyre
> The falcon cannot hear the falconer;
> Things fall apart; the centre cannot hold;
> Mere anarchy is loosed upon the world,
> The blood-dimmed tide is loosed, and everywhere
> The ceremony of innocence is drowned;
> The best lack all conviction, while the worst
> Are full of passionate intensity.
>
> Surely some revelation is at hand;
> Surely the Second Coming is at hand.
> The Second Coming! Hardly are those words out
> When a vast image out of Spiritus Mundi
> Troubles my sight: a waste of desert sand
> A shape with lion body and the head of a man,
> A gaze blank and pitiless as the sun,
> Is moving its slow thighs, while all about it
> Reel shadows of the indignant desert birds.
>
> The darkness drops again; but now I know
> That twenty centuries of stony sleep

Were vexed to nightmare by a rocking cradle,
And what rough beast, its hour come round at last,
Slouches towards Bethlehem to be born?

The bull version of the current environment, which I more or less embrace, is that the West will emerge from its current funk and eventually will deal with its malaise. America is America and it's always wrong to bet against her. The Europeans will eventually come up with a solution to the sovereign debt issue that may well include Greece's leaving the EU. The U.S. is gradually deleveraging and the economy is healthier than the bears admit. Valuations in the U.S. are cheap, and with stocks in Europe selling around book value they are really, truly cheap. We've been in a secular bear market since 1999 with compound negative real returns, and Treasury bonds have beaten equities since 1982. "Nobody knows nuthin'" about China, and we have two classes of forecasters: those who don't know, and those who don't know they don't know. So far at least the Chinese authorities seem to be successfully organizing a smooth, soft landing. Is China going to keep growing at 9–10% annually? No! But can the second biggest economy in the world crank out 6% a year real GDP growth for a while? Yes! India, Indonesia, Brazil, Mexico, and maybe even Nigeria are future growth dynamos.

A deleveraging America can probably do 2–3% real GDP growth for the next few years and even a sickly Europe could deliver 1%. With inflation of 3–4%, that generates decent nominal GDP growth. If so, the next move in the U.S. could be up 10–15% as the underweight public and institutions stampede back in. The stampede could become a panic as the momentum gang's computers go mad. Equity ratios and animal spirits are deeply depressed. Over the next year 20% upside is not inconceivable. However, the agony comes in that in this environment discovering cheap stocks is easy. The enormous difficulty is in finding cheap stocks that are safe, and in a high-frequency trading–dominated market like this one where divergences are minuscule may be virtually impossible.

Howard Marks is a really good thinker. He has always maintained that as an investor, you should focus more intently on the downside than the upside. Be very grudging, he says, about risking losing money. I agree. I don't want to lose capital. The darkest bears' vision of a second coming of a long cycle of wealth destruction and political chaos scares me. There is a beast out there. Nevertheless I'm spiritually inclined to think the next big move in stocks will be up—not down. However, America and

Europe are still bumbling along, and I am discouraged; I have reduced my net long from 70% to 50%. I like what I own, and so I sold an equal portion of everything, but I will move quickly if the outlook brightens or deteriorates. An improvement in the high frequency and house price numbers in America would be important signals as would more comity in the political rhetoric and action in both the U.S. and Europe.

Churchill was right. If you're going through hell, keep going!

Begin Thinking about Buying

The hell chart that is so easy to print now tells the story. Hell was from July 7 at 1,356 on the S&P 500 to 1,074 on October 4—a decline of 20% in three months with incredible volatility. There have been worse bear episodes in the spring of 1970, September of 1974, the Crash of 1987, and on some dark days in 2000, but this one really got to me. By late August I was down 9% and committed to not lose more than 10%, so I had reduced my net long to 20%. In the month of September my big contributors to performance were my large short positions in the S&P 500, Brazil, and the DAX index. My large long-standing position in global oil service stocks hurt a lot, as did China.

Perched on the ledge I am haunted by the exquisite, agonizing dilemma of the abyss versus the opportunity. The violent rally of the last few days, particularly the afternoon when the S&P 500 jumped 4.5% in 30 minutes on a Financial Times *story, highlights the vicious riptides of sentiment. Nevertheless I'm still inclined to play markets cautiously with a moderate net long. My problem has been that with about half of that net long concentrated in high-conviction positions in Thailand, China, and Indonesia I have been hurt by the manic investors' panic-selling last weeks of stocks in markets that haven't gone down yet. Both Thailand and Indonesia had a day last week when the entire market fell 8% to 9%. This kind of action is usually a sign that the end is near.*

■　■　■

October 3, 2011

I was in Europe last week, and all the smart and not-so-smart investors and business people I talked with were very, very bearish about Europe, America, China, and the world. *The Economist* cover this week of an ominous whirlpool spiraling into a black hole summed it up: "Until politicians actually do something about the world economy . . . be afraid."

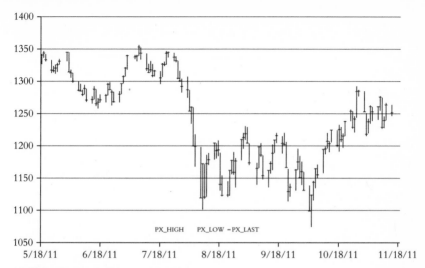

Hell S&P 500 5/18/11–11/14/11

Data source: Bloomberg

The U.S. media are equally gloom and doom. I sense we have either reached or are very close to the point where everyone, professionals and amateurs alike, know how grim the outlook is and how inept the politicians are. The old saying is that the point of maximum bearishness has to be the market bottom and we must be close.

However, Europe was sobering. The Authorities still don't get it, and while they fiddle, Europe and the world spiral towards a global double-dip recession with God only knows what social and financial consequences. Time is running out. The PMIs and ISMs confirm that Europe is already in recession, including Germany, where the most recent ZEW survey of confidence and expectations suggest the economy will be in a mild recession by Christmas. America is faltering, and China is beginning to look sickly. The bears are arguing China is on the verge of a hard landing centered on real estate with GDP growth collapsing to 2 or 3%. If that happens to the second largest economy, it will rock the world and commodity markets will continue to plummet. Another ominous sign is if credit market spreads continue to widen, although they are not back to 2008 levels. Even more serious and potentially disruptive, popular discord and discontent is growing in the night like a malignant tumor deep in the world's gut.

In Europe, as Gordon Brown wrote last week, it's becoming obvious "that the euro cannot survive in its present form; that many of our banks are close to insolvency, and that a much larger rescue fund—two, perhaps three trillion euros—is needed to stabilize the euro zone. Two trillion euros are needed just to recapitalize banks and finance the borrowing needs of Greece, Spain, Portugal, Ireland, and Italy until 2014." The expansion that the Bundestag approved last week of 440 billion euros is a pitiful drop in the bucket, and the inevitable next expansion will have to go through a whole new round of validation by the 17 parliaments. There is not even a G-20 meeting until early November. Meanwhile the clock keeps ticking, the economies continue weakening, and the size of the tumor keeps growing.

The European Authorities are still resisting the message. Angela Merkel, the German chancellor, met with Pope Benedict in Germany last week and commented afterwards: "We spoke about the financial markets and the fact that politicians should have power to make policy for the people and not be driven by markets." I sympathize with her, but it's not the current reality. The power should be with the people, but the truth is that the people have lost confidence in the politicians and they despise the bankers and hedge fund managers. There is intense anger in Europe that if the Greek sovereign debt is restructured at a 20% discount as is being proposed, the biggest beneficiaries will be the hedge funds who have bought the deeply discounted paper down 50%. The street mobs would happily guillotine the bankers and hedge fund managers, and the Hungarians have already proposed a revision of the terms of repayment of mortgages. It is also clear that the European governments are serious about a tax on financial transactions. Let's hope such a tax would put the high-frequency traders who terrorize us out of business.

The anger and rage at bankers and hedge fund managers is intensifying. Anticipate a 20-year secular bear market in the profits and compensation of the financial services industry including hedge funds and private equity. There is also deep discontent and disillusionment in Europe and around the world with free market capitalism and the political system. Socialism and communism failed 25 years ago, but now high unemployment, reduced social spending, grossly unequal distribution of incomes, political corruption, and self-dealing is festering. This is the true cause of the seemingly mindless demonstrations and riots from London to Wall Street to Bombay. As one person said to me: "With high hopes we elect them, and then they become corrupted by both the System with a capital S and the special interest groups." In Europe the Maastricht Treaty was poorly conceived and is impotent in the face of 17 different legislatures. In the U.S. the House of Representatives with its two-year term conceived of over 200 years ago may be structurally flawed for modern times. Then there is the curse of money and the lobbyists.

The question becomes have we reached the point of maximum bearishness and are valuations low enough? Has the market already discounted the earnings impact of a double-dip recession and a "new normal" of a decade of much slower world economic growth? The answer is no. We probably need one final break below the August and September lows in the big market averages. It also would be helpful if credit market spreads stabilized.

As we study it, sentiment is back to the levels that in the past have signaled important market lows. However, sentiment is a blunt instrument and not a short-term timing mechanism. More time could be required. As for valuations, let's assume that in a double-dip recession the S&P 500's earnings will fall 20–25% from 100 to 75 to 80. So at 14 to 15 times depressed profits, is the index at 1,100 cheap enough? I'm not sure. It depends on the slope of the eventual global economic recovery. However, based on some of the old tried and true valuation measures such as price to book (now at book value), price to cash flow (4.7 times), and price to sales (.57 of sales), European and Japanese stocks in particular are very cheap. The Euro Stoxx 50 yields 5.6%. The big U.S. multinationals are cheap but without the "very."

So what does an investor as opposed to a trader do? First of all you have to believe it's not the end of the world and that equities will survive. Bear markets don't last forever. In fact, markets around the world are a compressed spring. There will be gigantic moves in ravaged stocks, sectors, and markets. The pain trade is clearly up. The trader waits for the momentum to change and counts on his agility to jump in, while an investor gingerly puts some cash to work and starts buying the big-capitalization, high-quality, blue chip U.S. and European multinationals. I think a long-only manager should get to about 7–8% cash and a hedge fund a 40–50% net long. Both should go to church, the synagogue, the temple, or whatever and pray. As the old World War II song goes: "Praise the Lord and pass the ammunition and we'll all stay free." Begin thinking about buying.

Agnostic Optimist

In early October I screwed up my courage and went long by covering my shorts and buying more of my beloveds. It turned out we had a good month, posting a gain of almost 8%. Ending up to be down 3% for the year.

■ ■ ■

We live in a market world tortured by insane volatility. The S&P 500 (still the benchmark index for the world) swings 2–4% in an hour on a flimsy newspaper story; imagine what would happen if we got real news that was truly good or very bad. One of our correspondents maintains there is now a $500 billion short position in risk assets concentrated in European paper that could panic triggering an explosive melt-up. On the other hand, a trip back to the 2008–2009 lows is not inconceivable. As investors, we have to control our emotions and not be whipsawed by these violent, momentum-driven market spasms.

Every sophisticate I have talked with over the last week is looking for a pullback in the U.S. and European equity markets. Their view is that the rally from the lows of three weeks ago has reached its "bridge too far," and most have either reduced risk in their funds or plan to cut back. They are convinced that expectations for a Grand European plan in the next few weeks are wildly optimistic. It's a hard argument to deal with because although the European Authorities may come up with some bandages to stop the bleeding, in the long run the only lasting solution for Euroland is fiscal union and that seems revolutionary, remote, and extremely difficult to put together. Meanwhile in the U.S., political gridlock persists and anti–Wall Street demonstrations grow. Not a great combination, but ironically the economy seems okay.

I'm agnostic and have not sold or bought anything recently. In other words, I'm not convinced it is or isn't a bridge too far. My net long is now around 60%, and if I were a long-only manager, I would be holding 5–7% in cash. These are cowardly positions because you have to produce a great deal of alpha to outperform with moderate risk levels, and we have been in an investment world where asset, country, sector, and individual stock correlations are at record highs. There are a lot of different issues to consider. What follows is a summary of the good and the bad.

Encouraging signs in high-frequency numbers that U.S. economy is not double dipping

- Automobile sales and Ward's reports vehicle production schedules rising
- Retail sales and chain store sales last week above expectations (WMT, HD, etc.)
- Employment as shown by unemployment claims improving but unemployment still high
- Manufacturing and service PMIs firming and above 50
- Money supply and bank loans rising moderately as banks become more willing to lend
- Construction spending and orders continue to improve
- Two-thirds of companies that have reported Q3 earnings came in above expectations
- Financial obligations in U.S. have plunged $150 billion and relative to disposable personal income are at an 18-year low
- Corporate balance sheets incredibly strong

Discouraging signs world still slipping towards stagnation or a double-dip recession

- Europeans still talk and no action
- Threat of trade war with China, which could set off global trade war (like 1930s)
- Greeks still striking—they don't get it
- Super Committee apparently not making much progress
- Feuding and gridlock continues between Republicans and Democrats—jobs bill failed to pass Senate
- Congress unwilling to do anything about fiscal drag next year, which will be minus 200 bps of real GDP
- Social disorder growing, with Wall Street protests spreading around the world

- Political rhetoric in U.S. becoming more extreme
- J.P. Morgan points out there is "a striking gap" between hard activity and confidence survey data, with new orders declining and inventories in U.S., Europe, and Asia rising
- Leading indicators, particularly business and consumer confidence, around the world still generally soggy (German ZEW)
- Evidence mounts Europe is slipping into recession with not just southern Europe but Germany and France now in recession
- G-20 meeting last weekend warning about time running out
- Greece spreads soaring and banks balking at 50% haircut
- S&P lowers Spain's credit rating and downgrades Italian banks
- Bank stocks across Europe still weak with huge capital needs
- Germans signal on Monday to expect no short-term magic solution
- Eventual solution has to be fiscal unification of Euroland and a 2–3 trillion dollar bank package

Asia problematical

- Japan has become sluggish again, with surveys reporting widespread corporate pessimism
- China data this week still pretty good with real estate bubble worries, but soft landing still the most likely outcome with real GDP of 7–9% next year
- Chinese Sovereign Wealth Fund buying banks, inflation ebbing, rate cut coming?
- Asian and most other EM countries' fiscal, monetary, and economic positions far stronger than in 2007–2008 and companies have much healthier balance sheets
- Emerging market CBs, with exception of BOJ, able to cut rates and last week six EM CBs, from Brazil to Russia, cut rates

So what am I looking at that would motivate me to raise my invested position, or conversely, to reduce it? I'm looking for first, real, tangible progress in drafting a credible plan for the European crisis. The conference this weekend has to address the size and leverage of the rescue fund (two to three trillion needed), a program for recapitalization of the banking sector, and a 50% haircut on Greek debt.

Second, I need a continued improvement in the high-frequency economic numbers around the world, which would signal odds of a double dip have diminished significantly. The global economy, the social order, and the financial markets would be severely damaged by a double-dip recession. Third, movement towards a Grand Bargain in the U.S. that raises the Social Security and Medicare retirement ages five years, cuts the defense budget to 2.5% of GDP, raises the tax burden on the very rich, deals with the mortgage overhang, and eliminates the 200 bps of fiscal drag for 2012. Fourth, getting the demonstration campers off the streets and calmed down would be helpful.

If progress on some or all of these began to emerge, equity markets could soar. As mentioned, a blowout rally and a 20–25% cyclical bull market in the next year are conceivable. The secular bear market would still be intact. If the political leadership fails in both Europe and the U.S. and the economy stagnates, equity markets could break through the lows of August and September and could be down 20% a year from now. The agony continues! I'm still inclined to think the near-term odds are with the optimists.

My Bet Is that the Rally Is Still a Work in Process

October 31, 2011

isk markets have now rallied for four weeks in a row, and last week global equities soared 4.5%. Copper, high yield, and spreads correlated. Now the commentary from the wise men is that the program that eventually emerged from last week's European summit is another lame effort. Most of the advice seems to be that risk markets have overreacted and are overbought, and that exposure, particularly to equities, should be reduced. They may well be right. It's a hard argument to refute after the incredible run the equity markets have had in October, which has only been matched on three other occasions in modern times.

However, I'm not so sure I want to cut back on risk yet. I wouldn't give the new European program an A, but I think it does merit a B minus. Others think it deserves an F. The lead editorial this week in *The Economist*, the best, most thoughtful publication in the world, concludes: "For all the back slapping and brave words, Europe's leaders have once again failed. There will be more crises, and further summits. By the time they settle on a solution that works, the costs will have risen still further."

My guess is markets were expecting a C at best and probably another dud.

Without wading into all the fine print, my view is that nevertheless it is a definite step in the right direction, and I suspect the specifics will be worked out satisfactorily. My partner Amer Bisat, who spent 10 years at the IMF, tells me the staff negotiations that go on after the initial announcement generally proceed well because there is a bias to make progress. He was involved in a number of such negotiations. He considers it very significant that the new chairman of the ECB said the central bank would continue to buy Italian sovereigns. He'd better be as good as his words because Italian bonds sold off on Friday.

There are two other factors that are moving markets. First, the U.S. economy is doing considerably better than expected. Over the last month there has been a preponderance of encouraging statistics, ranging from individual company comments (Caterpillar) to various activity indicators. Last week capital goods shipments, credit card delinquencies, corporate profits, inventory levels, consumer confidence, and consumer spending all exceeded expectations. ECRI's leading index rose for the second straight week. M2 in the U.S. has surged almost 20%, and M3 in Europe is finally accelerating.

Admittedly the data on housing including the Case–Shiller index were downbeat, real disposable personal income in the U.S. fell again, and the high-frequency data from Europe are glum. The Super Committee continues to report stalemate, which is very discouraging. Finally the floods in Thailand may be disrupting supply chains in the world economy, and an inventory adjustment is lingering over much of emerging Asia.

Nevertheless, the consensus forecasts of the soothsayers for the fourth quarter in the U.S. have risen to 2.5% for real GDP and to 5% for nominal GDP. There has always been a high correlation between the stock market in October–November and the strength of the holiday season's retail sales in both America and Europe. The violence of the current rally will reinforce ordinary people's view that Wall Street is crazy, but subliminally it will increase their propensity to spend. Business also will notice and it may push them to spend some of their huge hoard of cash on capital spending and even to step-up hiring.

The rally last week and its future over the next couple of months is very much about positioning. The major prime brokers tell me that about 20% of the hedge funds on their platforms were net short as of midweek. The ISI hedge fund surveys taken on Wednesday showed that hedge funds overall reduced their net long over the previous five trading days to a new low since March 2009. I know that several of the most respected prop trading funds were net short Thursday morning and actually had losses for the week. The ISI surveys also indicate that long-only managers have been cutting their long positions and raising cash aggressively over the last four weeks. The public, sick of these shenanigans, has checked out.

Hedge fund and long-only managers have been struggling in this very difficult and stressful environment. They mostly are lagging their benchmarks and are in the red for the year; in some cases, the famous are deep underwater. With two months to go until year-end and sullen, restless clients, they are feeling a lot of pressure. After the terror of chaotic, panic declines, they now are suffering the new indignity of being underinvested in the biggest monthly rally in history. We always knew Mr. Market was a sadist, but this time he has been unusually ingenious and cruel. Investment managers know they have got to get their acts together by year-end. I don't think they will leap in on top of this spike, but I do suspect they will be looking feverishly for opportunities to get more invested and certainly will be buying the dips unless the world changes. As I mentioned in my last letter, my experience is that clients are reasonably tolerant of owning too much in a falling market but get very nasty when you miss a rising one—particularly a giant.

Of course there are risks. The U.S. economy could falter again. Unemployment could rise after the holiday season. China could stumble or the rise in oil prices could abort consumption around the world. And then there is the enduring nightmare that Europe's latest fix is not a fix after all. Watch credit spreads. Meanwhile it looks like France has tipped into recession, joining the other half dozen continental economies that are already contracting. Sitting here in Greenwich in an October snowstorm that has shut off power, roads, telephones, and heat, I'm sensitive to the unexpected.

But also meditate on what would happen to markets if the Super Committee improbably rose to greatness, broke its stalemate, and proposed a Social Security retirement age of 70, an age modification for Medicare, a cut in the defense budget to 2.5% of GDP over three to five years, a tax increase on the rich, and closing of the obvious corporate and individual loopholes. Or maybe no tax increase and an elimination of tax relief on carried interest, mortgages, charitable contributions, capital gains etc., which would be the same thing and would assuage the Occupy Wall Street crowd.

Anyway, I'm keeping my hopes up and my net long elevated. In America, tech both new and old, oil service and natural gas, and the big-cap, industrial multinationals. I think the data from China suggest a "delicate" landing, a 7–8% real GDP growth path, and a gradual decline in inflation. In real estate, where the bears are focused, there may be an "elegant" fall but no bust. My hunch is that after a long spell in the doldrums, the Chinese markets are going to fly as the gigantic short position from Western hedge funds panics. I own the despised H shares, Hong

Kong, MSCI China (more consumer stocks), and Hong Kong luxury property courtesy of Ted Bigman, the best equity real estate investor in the world.

I also have and hold Indonesia, Thai banks, cheap unloved Korea, and some Taiwan stocks. The big, long-term story across Asia is the rise of domestic demand. The Asian countries have tiny budget deficits, current account surpluses, and modest debt as a percent of GDP. Their central banks have plenty of room to cut their official interest rates. Australia could be close to easing, and other emerging economies such as Brazil have a similar luxury. Incidentally lower relative commodity and particularly oil prices are very bullish for Asian growth. I'm also tempted by Japan, although other than the cheapness of its stocks, it is not easy to become excited.

I suspect for the time being "in the affairs of men" there could be a virtuous circle feedback effect, and that the rally is a work in process. Often wrong, always in doubt.

The Truth Will Set You Free but Chardonnay Isn't Bad Either

*A*t this point I am not ready to pile on more risk because the European credit markets and even foreign exchange spreads are signaling distress, even extreme distress. Europe could be on the brink of a funding crisis, and in an interconnected world banking system the contagion would affect everyone. Thus the disconnect between credit and equities is very disconcerting. One or the other has to give. We all know the violence of the volatility that would unleash.

It's all very confusing because meanwhile I am feeling better and better about risk markets in general and equities in particular for a number of reasons. My reasons are as follows in no particular order. All of these events don't have to happen for markets to work higher—only one of two would be enough to frighten the bears. I think there is a reasonable chance that will happen.

First, sentiment remains incredibly bearish, both anecdotally and on the basis of our indicators. According to the ISI survey, hedge funds cut their net long positions again last week. The doom and gloom chorus is louder and more strident than ever. Between now and year-end the pain trade is up.

Second, the U.S. economy is continuing to do surprisingly well in the face of a deluge of disconcerting bad news at home and abroad. Last week unemployment claims, railcar loadings, bank loans, retail surveys, and earnings for the S&P 500 all had modest up-ticks consistent with 2.0–2.5% real GDP growth. This past Tuesday the retail sales report was very positive, and lower inflation is improving purchasing power. The fourth-quarter real GDP could come in as high as 3%. The odds of a double dip continue to diminish.

Third, China is the second largest economy in the world and the dynamo. A hard landing in China is a key factor in the bears' case. Last week China signaled credit easing as local currency lending in October soared to 586 billion yuan up from 470 billion in September and exceeding all economists' estimates. Last weekend at the Asia Pacific Economic forum, IMF managing director Zhu Min said China was heading for a "soft landing from inflationary growth" and that sustainable growth was "about 8%." He and China's President Hu Jintao asserted imports would rise, inflation was declining, bad debts at banks were lower, and that the property bubble was under control.

These statements by very senior officials are a big deal as they indicate the Authorities are moving their principal focus to stimulating and maintaining economic growth instead of on curbing inflation and pricking the luxury real estate bubble. That's welcome news for the world and for China and for my China positions. I hope it makes the shorts very nervous, but they seem to have nerves of steel. Also note that Brazil, Russia, and Indonesia have actually cut rates.

Fourth, just maybe there is some progress in Europe or at least the crisis has been pushed further into the future. The appointment of two highly regarded technocrats in Italy and Greece is a step in the right direction, and Draghi, the new chairman of the ECB, seems a major improvement over Jean-Claude Trichet, who seemed oblivious to the recession the continent is drifting into. However, Frau Merkel and the other leaders still seem to be content to keep kicking the can down the road, and I have to admit the situation remains very fragile. France is the key. Watch the spreads on French debt. If they keep rising, head for shore.

Fifth, I am an optimist. My sense is that the American people are beginning to understand the dimensions of the deficit problem and that something has to be done. A consensus is developing that the Social Security retirement age has to be raised meaningfully and that Medicare has to be reduced. Even some of the wealthy agree their taxes should be increased, and there are broad agreement tax loopholes such as carried interest and corporate deductions that have to be changed. Everyone knows the defense budget at over 5% of GDP with spending more than the entire rest of the world combined has to be cut big time.

Thus I can't believe the Super Committee is going to permit itself to flop, but the expert commentary from the top-ranked Washington gurus is that there is a 50% chance that it will be unable to come up with anything at all and no chance whatsoever for a "Grand Bargain." I'm an

optimist because this would be such a pathetic outcome and so embar-
rassing for the members in particular and politicians in general I can't
believe they would let his happen. I'm willing to bet they pull something
out of the hat, and there is even one chance in five they do a transforming deal. That would be very bullish for America and the world.

I'm still running a moderate net long in the mid-40s. Same old stories
in the US: tech, oil service, industrial manufacturing, medium and small
caps. Love Asia: China plus Korea, Indonesia, Taiwan, Hong Kong, and
even flood-drenched Thai banks. The banks in the U.S. and particularly
Europe will rocket if risk goes back on, but I'm not strong and brave
enough at this point to endure the volatility. My major short positions are
in French and German equities. France because it could be the next animal to be attacked and because its banks are so imperiled and Germany
because a breakup of the euro would destroy its competitive position.

We all have to control our mood swings. Volatility is turning us into
manic depressives. Last week I was tempted to add after the first two days
but didn't. Then I was plunged into terror by the collapse on Wednesday.
Thursday and Friday the clouds lifted some and a sharp rally occurred.
We have to keep remembering the right thing to do is to have a view and
then buy weakness and cut back some on strength.

Investing in a World Lit Only by Fire

November 29, 2011

I have been too optimistic about our leaders and about the resilience of markets. Both the Super Committee and the Europeans have failed to deal with the crucial issues of deficits, leverage, and entitlements. Today's powerful rally is impressive, but I fear it's a flash in the pan. The financial markets are relentless and so far have refused to be appeased with soft words and hollow promises of future cuts in wages and benefits. I think Frau Merkel and the German Finance Minister Schaeuble are right that it will take a deeper crisis to create the popular support for true austerity. In the meantime, although the U.S. economy is continuing to strengthen, the recovery is built on shifting sand. Across the pond, while the leaders dither, Europe is slipping deeper into recession territory. The odds of a double dip have increased significantly.

As a result, I'm staying close to shore with around a 30% net long position, but I'm not going net short. There are just too many uncertainties. There's an old saying that may have relevance today: "He who knows not and knows that he knows not is a wise man." I hope I'm being wise and not just cowardly in hovering near harbor. Fortunately or unfortunately, experience teaches that the likelihood of a market decline is inversely proportional to the size of your cash position and the lowness of your net long, and the likelihood of the decline being reversed is in direct proportion to the amount of selling you do during the decline. Positions you want to buy in the decline will go up and positions you sold in anticipation of the decline also will go up. Hedges will cost you money. The reasons for the above will only become clear after the ensuing rally carries the market substantially higher while you underperform. Mr. Market is a perverted sadist, and he has thoroughly enjoyed himself this year.

The problem with all this fiddling by the Authorities is that, as it goes on, the global economy is tottering. Decreasing economic activity and fiscal drag are a lethal combination. Anecdotal data ranging from bulk carrier loadings to capital spending and hiring budgets are faltering. The European coincident indicator is signaling recession. Confidence in Asia, Europe, and America is clearly being affected by the incompetence and uncertainty. The Bloomberg U.S. Consumer Comfort Index has reached minus 50 or less in 9 of the past 10 weeks for the first time in its 26-year history. I find it incredible that with the savings rate having fallen back to around 3.5%, U.S. retail sales during the Thanksgiving weekend rose 16%. Where is the money for this spending splurge coming from? However, the National Retail Foundation, hardly an unbiased party, is forecasting that for the full holiday season sales will rise a mere 2.8% this year compared with a 5.2% gain last year.

So many words, theories, and remedies are on display about the political malaise in Europe and the U.S. that I have no inclination to add to them. It does seem, however, that as of this moment the European Authorities led by Merkel, Schaeuble, and ECB Chairman Draghi want tighter budget discipline and reforms in the sick countries and basically an Austrian model solution. They appear to recognize that the markets will see through and disdain the cardboard remedies. Pouring more fiscal gasoline on the fire hasn't worked, so I'm sympathetic to an Austrian, Hegel-type solution, but we have to recognize that a stiff dose of austerity and a global double dip are very risky. Occupy Wall Street may seem like child's play compared with the social disorder to come. I remember in the stagflation and paralysis of the 1970s in America the burning cities and the Kent State massacre. Admittedly, the additional issue that time was Vietnam and the draft, but on the other hand there wasn't the inequality of the 99% and the rage against the bankers.

What would Keynes say about all this? Seems to me he would be so shocked by the fiscal deficits and mad spending practices that Europe and America engaged in during the expansion that he would be rendered mute. Keynesian economics firmly advocates surpluses during prosperity and deficits to revive the beast during recessions. Even Paul Krugman seems to have changed his tune. Economics are what economists do.

We are where we are, and it's not pretty. I don't find either equities or fixed income enticing enough to warrant a major position. As for commodities, the only consistently profitable extractive industry is dentistry, and currencies are dominated by the crazies, with 20-to-1 leverage and tight stops. There is nothing the matter with being defensive and in cash when there are no compelling values and enormous uncertainty. On the dark days I even wonder about where you hold the cash. The uncomfort-able issue is we are supposed to be investment managers and we get paid fees to make money. However, now seems to be a time to concentrate on the preservation of capital and maintaining its spending power. Like they say, worry about the return of the money, not the return on the money. It's not a lot of fun investing in a world lit only by fire, but don't despair—opportunities will develop.

Private Equity

I am on a board of a $2 billion foundation and last year at the fall meeting the investment adviser proposed that we gradually move from a 12% allocation in private equity (PE) to a 30% position. The fund was as high as 28% in PE in 2006 with a net return of over 20%, and the adviser then strongly recommended cutting the position in half. The board agreed, and the adviser implemented by actually selling the positions in a number of the funds at a premium. Thus the board was receptive to this new allocation but a number of us wondered if 30% in an illiquid asset wasn't too high. It was pointed out that in 2008 and 2009 endowments and pension funds with high PE allocations suffered painful liquidity crises. I offered to do some work. Here is my report.

■ ■ ■

December 2, 2011

I have talked with a number of people about private equity (PE) most of whom are friends to a greater or lesser degree and all of whom are serious, professional investors responsible for other people's money. I told them I was trying to refine my view of PE as an asset class for the next 5 to 10 years in the context of the appropriate asset allocations for a $2 billion fund that was an active, multi-asset investor with a long horizon, real return, growth objective. I did tell them that the fund had an annual payout requirement. I was not more specific than that.

What did they think, I asked, of PE in terms of the potential returns over the next five to seven years in a difficult world—a world lit only by fire? What were the environmental risks of the asset class as well as the manager selection hazards? Was the next year to 18 months a propitious time to increase the commitment to PE? What kind of absolute and risk-adjusted returns could be expected from PE versus other asset classes over the next five years? Most, I think, were quite candid and open. I took notes and the summaries of their remarks are in italics, but, obviously, these are not transcribed comments. Please, by all means, keep their views to yourself as some could be seriously embarrassed if they became attributed.

■   ■   ■

Seventy-Year-Old Retired Partner, Giant Private Equity Fund: Major issue is: Are you willing to suffer 10 years of illiquidity for superior long-term performance? Big funds are a leveraged bet on public equity markets, and size is the enemy of performance. Big Firm has recruited a very large number of extremely bright, very ambitious, capable young people, but can all this talent be harnessed? Their expectations are excessive, and he worries the environment at Big Firm is too elitist and euphoric about PE. Nevertheless Big Firm is well managed with marketing, client relationships, and deal analysis meticulously organized. He wonders if previous returns are sustainable as there are so many new PE firms trying to get into the business and so much money coming in. He was just back from Middle East seeing big sovereign wealth funds. I sense this man whom I know well is uneasy about the size of Big Firm and he was evasive about future returns.

■   ■   ■

This Man Is a Former Managing Director of Morgan Stanley and Trustee of a Major University and Chairman of the Investment Committee of Its Endowment: The university's $8 billion endowment has 30% in PE and is comfortable at that level. Doesn't hire big firms. Uses regional, smaller, medium-sized, specialist firms that are proven business doctors. Says good old Southern boy and business school relationships help a lot with manager selection. Doesn't really consider macro environment. The trustees of the school include the governor and some of them get nervous with PE in bear markets. He wonders if so many new entrants will compete away future returns. Worries entry of U.S. state funds and sovereign wealth funds will overwhelm the PE environment with easy, "stupid" money.

■   ■   ■

Former President of a Major Investment Management Firm, Now a Partner of a Private Wealth Management Firm, on 12 Different Investment Committees and at One Time Chairman of Investment Committee of One of the Largest Endowments in the World and Has Run the Endowment for an Elite, Rich College for 15 Years With Heavy Emphasis on PE. Results So Spectacular They Gave Him an Honorary Degree. Conservative, Nervous Investor with a Magnificent Record: Still very positive on PE as an asset class and remains convinced it is the best asset class. Expects 500 bps above public equities next five to seven years. Amherst still has over 60% of endowment in PE. Total alignment of interest between investors and managers so he has no use for PE firms that have gone public or are bank owned. Only invests in PE firms whose business model is to turn around troubled companies. No LBO firms and avoids firms that do financial transactions. Access of a PE firm to a pool of professional managers to insert into acquired companies is very important. Not worried about deflation and debt because low interest rates reduce PE borrowing costs. Stick with the best firms but getting entrée to them is crucial.

Emphasized that before you make a big commitment to PE you have to be sure board and institution are willing to suffer 10 years of illiquidity and extreme volatility in one- to three-year returns in exchange for superior long term performance. Boards of both Harvard and Amherst after years of wonderful returns from PE got very apprehensive in 2008–2009. Says it would take five to six years to put together a $1–2 billion diversified PE portfolio from scratch. Periodic inflows and outflows of cash stemming from unscheduled drawdowns, uncertain timing, and from (money vs. stock) of distributions can be troublesome for a trust or foundation. Because of the business, accounting, and legal complexities (claw-backs, etc.) you need a professional staff to monitor a portfolio of 20 or 30 PE firms.

■ ■ ■

Chairman of a Giant Hedge Fund Empire That He Built from Scratch, Experienced, Sophisticated Investor: Doesn't believe in PE. Too illiquid and too much competition and you can't effectively hedge it. His firm has had some big hits in Chinese PE because of connections, but he seems to wonder if it's repeatable. Thinks success and riches seem to spoil PE guys eventually. Not a fan of the big firms. Critical of big lavish birthday parties. Stable of well-selected hedge funds still the best way to go but you have to realize that you're always going to have some that don't perform. Wonders if big PE firms aren't just a leveraged bet on public equity market. Says Carlisle has over 200 managing directors. He thinks we are in a secular bear market and is bearish about the world.

■   ■   ■

Manager of the Endowment Fund of a Large University. His Record Has Been Spectacular and He Is Universally Viewed as a Pioneer in Asset Allocation: Believes in PE and is raising endowment's allocation to 40% of portfolio but admits previous commitments to PE and shrinkage of endowment portfolio from losses and annual withdrawal formula has to some extent forced his asset allocation higher. Convinced satisfactory returns in nonpublic markets characterized by incomplete information and illiquidity are only achievable by selecting superior managers. Monitoring PE funds more productive use of your professional staff than searching for long-only performers where differentials between top quintile and median is 200 bps long-term vs. 500–600 bps in PE. The whole game is to get into top quintile funds as they alone produce returns sufficient to compensate for PE's greater risk and illiquidity. PE as an asset class does not deliver superior risk-adjusted returns to its investors. Over the long run PE as an asset class has a lower net annual return than public equities. Don't use PE firms that are owned by anyone other than the managers themselves and is particularly disdainful of investment banks, commercial banks, and publicly owned firms.

If you are going to go big in PE you have to truly recognize there will be enormous volatility in one- and five-year returns. Vintage year diversification is essential. Best firms stay good and remain good even after they get big. Mediocre firms stay mediocre and often deteriorate. Just being in the asset class won't do. PE firms that concentrate on improving the operating performance of their portfolio companies consistently do far better than those that just leverage up cheap or troubled companies. Buying cheap cyclical companies often doesn't work because it's hard to sell them and you are very vulnerable to cyclical swings in the economy. Has little use for LBO firms as opposed to PE. Investors in LBO firms are not compensated for the extreme risk of leverage and immense illiquidity. LBO investments in the absence of value-adding activities by the transaction sponsor simply increase the risk profile of the company. He is also increasing the endowment's hedge fund allocation, and he is now disenchanted with timberland and farmland. Working on putting more money into PE in emerging markets but currency adds a whole additional level of risk.

It's a little hard to understand where he is right now. He remarks that a fair amount of the "observed" diversification effect provided by PE comes from the infrequent valuations of illiquid assets. Wonders if you can count on the PE firms' valuations anyway. He ruminates that big-cap, high-quality equities particularly in the U.S. are a great place, maybe the best place to be, but the endowment has a relatively small allocation to them and a big allocation to PE. I was surprised he wasn't more enthusiastic about PE considering the growing size of his commitment. He is bearish on risk assets and thinks the S&P 500 is going to test the 2009 low.

■ ■ ■

CEO and CIO of a Medium-Sized PE Fund Owned by an Investment Bank. A Very Good, Smart Guy: Being aligned with an investment bank is a major negative in fund raising. Everyone now knows not to give money to a PE firm run by an investment bank. Claims investment bank relationship gives him great access through investment bankers into info about talented business managers who are available to hire to run portfolio companies. PWM clients of bank are developing substantial interest in PE from their wealthy clients who are fed up with stock market volatility. These people think PE is a great way to get rich and MS gives them a substantial trailer fee. However, he is hearing complaints from his PWM investors about long delays in getting tax info causing complexity and multiple filings. Rise of auctions for deals is a negative because it will compete away returns. Also worries a bad stock market will make it much tougher to exit holdings at a good price.

■ ■ ■

Experienced, Honest PE Managing Director of a Large Fund: Investment world in a sustained period of volatility. Banks will continue to lend but will do so cautiously. Middle market refinancing needs will accelerate in 2012 and beyond, but absolute rates will remain low and reputable firms will be able to borrow at attractive rates but using reduced leverage. He seems surprisingly negative on investment environment and said mean reversion would suggest that equities will outperform the liquid, leveraged finance asset classes.

■ ■ ■

Former Chairman of a Large Commercial Bank Now Chairman of a Major Foundation: Reducing PE from 20% to 10% in DD foundation. Too much money currently committed to PE but uninvested. Unhealthy that PE firms have to spend that money or give it back. Deal premiums soaring. Everything big has been picked over and is very competitive. Fees are too high in a future world where investments returns are mid to high single digits. Another significant negative for a foundation is delay in year-end accounting values which are needed for five percent rule. Later said he was talking mostly about US PE and to a lesser extent European PE. He likes emerging market PE and says it is a different matter. Less competition but a high risk game what with corruption, currency risk, poor auditing. Plans to do some PE direct investing himself when he retires which is December 31.

■ ■ ■

Two CIOs of Large State Pension Funds, Bureaucrats In Good Sense of the Word, Worried About Job Security but Quite Sophisticated and Cynical. As One Said, "I've Heard Every Investment Pitch Known to Man at Least 10 Times": They desperately need to show asset class investments with the potential of delivering 8–9% annual returns to get local press, unions, and politicians off their backs. After the last 12 years it is hard to justify such returns with public equities and fixed income, but with PE they can indicate that possibility. Their trustees are unsophisticated, unpaid, and desperately want to stay out of negative publicity and trouble. They also want to avoid PE firms that flaunt their wealth and Schwartzman's birthday party was cited. But they also want famous, large, brand name PE funds, which is inconsistent. They claim they are fee conscious and say they will insist on much lower fees for commitments $500 million and up. Will do the same with hedge funds but complain the big long-short hedge funds that go for alpha and promised 8–10% annual returns are not delivering. Both CIOs were very concerned about blowups and short-term volatility in hedge funds and PE, which could cost them their jobs. They are hiring consultants or using funds of funds particularly with hedge funds but also PE to insulate themselves. Both said they are planning to raise their allocation from 5% to 20% over the next few years.

■ ■ ■

Wealthy Individual Who Manages Approximately $6 Billion of Family-Related Trusts. Tough Clientele as They Are All Related and Are Very Critical. As One Relative at His 65th Birthday Party Said in His Toast, "Jack's a Great Guy *and Being Related to Him Has Cost Me $50 Million Dollars in the Last Three Years"*: Jack has very little in PE today but is considering raising his allocation very substantially because he likes the control PE has and the current opportunity to buy companies cheap. He has long argued that professional management in big companies has different motivations than shareholders. They focus on buying back stock to raise ROE to justify higher compensation rather than paying dividends. Also says, "The process of control is an offset to a sluggish economy. Look at the job Blackstone has done managing their hotel properties." Thinks investing in distressed debt is an interesting way to get into PE as you often end up with PE. Also believes buying the stocks of Blackstone and KKR, and maybe even Fortress may be the best way of all to invest in PE. Incredibly cheap and disdained. Recognizes change in the tax rate on carried interest earnings will be a big negative but is probably already in the price. These stocks are like buying the fund package and having liquidity. However, he would not invest more than 30% of his assets in PE. Broad diversification in a troubled world is essential. Wouldn't want to own 50% of anything.

■ ■ ■

Influential Asset Allocation Strategist, TV Personality, Author of Books on Asset Allocation: The long lockup and illiquidity make PE difficult for the wealthy individuals (PWM) he advises but he finds a surprising amount of interest. These people disenchanted with stock market volatility and intrigued with big names in PE like the cocktail party, name-dropping cachet for them of being able to say they are a partner with Henry Kravis or Steve. However, PWM clients don't have access to big star funds. Instead banks try to motivate PWM brokers with fat trailer fee to sell in-house funds. Theoretically, since PE involves highly firm-specific investments in products, people, or businesses, it should have a low correlation with public equity markets and risk. Thinks wealthy individuals ($5–$10 million) should have 4–6% in PE.

■ ■ ■

Former Partner of KKR and Very Successful, Highly Regarded PE Investor Now Retired but Still Dabbles: He continues to believe PE is the best asset class because of the alignment of interests and the ability of company managements to take a longer-term view and not have to worry about quarterly earnings reports, analysts, and market reactions. Four hundred basis points above public equities after fees is a monumental achievement.

Thinks the giant firms have become autocratic and muscle bound and that they will not be the first quartile performers of the future. Points out that fixed fees have become such a major source of income for the previously successful firms that they may no longer have the intensity and motivation needed to excel. If he were doing it, he says he would concentrate on medium-sized, middle market PE firms. Although the current environment is challenging with so much money trying to get to work, he thinks there must be excellent opportunities in smaller companies. Getting deal flow is essential to the success of a firm. Agrees with Swensen that cyclical companies are troublesome and is skeptical about emerging market PE.

■ ■ ■

Very Smart, Very Wealthy Professional Who Runs His Family Money and a Foundation that Has Done Extremely Well With Big PE Investments: Has invested in PE for 20 years and is in both the big firms and also insists on co-investment rights. Has done well but is finding fees a hurdle and says he always seems to be getting capital calls when he least wants them. Size truly is the enemy of performance. Also being charged a fee on uninvested money irritates him. Now is trying to move more to medium-sized firms. Major attraction of them for him is that often they give him co-investment rights on certain deals. No fees on co-investments and much easier to follow. Very time intensive, he says, to identify really sustainable mid-sized firms but thinks they can deliver 500–600 bps above public equities.

■ ■ ■

Chairman and CIO of a Large Fund of Hedge Funds, She Is on Six Investment Committees of Prestigious Foundations and Endowments, Smart and Sophisticated: She also is skeptical about the big firms being able to sustain first quartile performance. Showed me results of one large foundation. Their public equity for the past 10 years has been about 100 bps annually better than the S&P, and PE has been about 100 under the S&P and that is after a huge winner in Google. Wasn't Google really venture capital? For the previous five years PE was 400 under the S&P. Some years ago she was a partner of a giant PE firm and found the head guy "very difficult" and she indicates that the firm is principally just a huge asset-gathering machine. Their connections with world leaders and the rich and famous have helped them in the past to get assets and deals. Will it keep working? Fundamentally she thinks hedge funds are better, more flexible, and less illiquid than PE, but after all she runs a fund of funds.

■ ■ ■

CIO of a Giant Family Office of a Man Who Made $10 Billion in an Internet Investment. Owner of Family Office Is Capricious and Likes to Make Billion Dollar PE Investments on a Stand-Alone Basis. Results Have Been Disastrous in One Case and Only Fair in the Others. Co-Investment Rights Are Important in This Case and Owner Is Receptive to Technology and Internet PE Deals: Firm would like to do $100 million pieces if they could get into best PE firms, which they believe are no longer the giants. Also are very troubled by high fee structure of PE. Co-investment rights very important to them, and I sense owner resents PE titans, who he thinks are pompous asses. Probably the firm is going to do PE internally to avoid the fee hurdle. Owner seems to think he, as a famous entrepreneur, will generate good deal flow and is confident (despite his previous setbacks) he can identify winners. Firm is building a staff of analysts. Good luck to them.

■ ■ ■

My Comments: I wonder if in their search for returns PE funds are making a mistake in doing an increasing amount of venture capital–type investing by buying into tech and Internet companies that need early-stage financing. I would call it the Facebook and Groupon syndrome. PE firms should stick to PE investing and not become high-risk venture capital investors in drag. Venture capital as an asset class has had no return, zero for the last decade, and even the best firms have struggled. Also PE firms should be careful not to be seduced into financial transactions or acquisitions where they assume the role of a merchant bank. Pure financial engineering is unattractive as providing financing represents a commodity activity with low barriers of entry.

LBO investing, as David Swensen has pointed out, is inherently very risky because of the leverage. Leverage is what killed the Morgan Stanley real estate funds. Incidentally, Carlisle on a new real estate fund that it is currently marketing has raised the hurdle rate to 8% and reduced the fixed fee to 75 bps. I think we are a third of the way through a secular bear market in the investment management, hedge fund, and PE businesses. Fees and compensation are coming down and will continue to come down. I like that our adviser is now showing us PE funds that concentrate on middle market companies, use little leverage, and have hurdle rates. We just looked at four mid-market, Scandinavian PE funds. Two had hurdle rates of 8%, one of 6%, and one zero. When challenged, the zero guy said take it or leave it.

My conclusion is that since the trust has a long-term horizon and is not obsessed with liquidity considerations, we should raise our PE allocation significantly but to 30%, not 50%. Bear in mind that the allocation will drift higher either through superior performance or as Yale's did. I'm still a stock guy in my heart and soul and I cherish liquidity, but I do understand the appeal of PE.

The other issue for me is: Are we totally confident in our PE adviser and his firm? Are we sure of his longevity in the business and the sustainability of his firm's excellence? Does it have access outside of Europe? Middle-size firms that will be the future winners in China, the Americas, and the emerging markets will be hard to identify for Charles. Note that PE in China is all about reputation and knowing the right people.

Another Tsunami

December 14, 2011

*N*ow I'm back to the mundane complexities of the battle.

The European Summit last week was a B+ but not the transforming event some hoped for and the markets at this point are giving it a B−. The Chinese CPI slowed to 4.2% and pork prices continued to decline suggesting further CPI weakness opening the door to rate cuts. However, the Shanghai Composite continues to act very poorly and is on the verge of a breakdown. In New York, a high Chinese government official told a small group that China had an income disparity problem just as the U.S. did except that it was 2% vs. 98% instead of 1% vs. 99%.

To me the most frightening recent revelation was that the Iranians have the technology expertise that they were able to discover and successfully break into the command and control the guidance system of one of our drones flying 50,000 feet over Iran, divert it, and land it without a scratch. It is a treasure trove for the Iranians and anyone they decide to share it with. This particular drone was highly sophisticated and had supposedly infallible stealth plus a camera system that could see through clouds. It also had automatic firewalls that immediately return it to base if an electronic threat occurs, and a failsafe to blow it up if it doesn't respond. It probably carried Sparrow drones. Obviously nothing worked as advertised. The Israelis must also be very concerned.

Anyway, I remain agnostic about markets. I can make a plausible case for 20% up or 20% down. For the time being, the key is to watch the spreads on Italian and French sovereigns. They will provide the ultimate grade the fixed income markets give last week's European developments. Contentious comments from the Bundesbank haven't helped. I still think the U.S. and Asian markets are the most attractive, but I'm not ready to put on more risk.

The U.S. has many inherent advantages over other areas of the world for economic growth and investment. Among them:

- U.S. vs. Fractured Eurozone—unity, one language, Constitution
- Good Demographics—growing population
- Mobility of Labor Markets
- Cheap Energy Sources—natural gas fracking
- Undervalued Currency
- Entrepreneurial Culture—Silicon Valley, availability of funding for startups
- Best Universities
- Many of Best Companies—multinationals
- Deep Liquid Capital Markets—fairest markets, insider trading convictions, Raj
- Rule of Law in Commerce and Investment
- America Will Be Biggest Oil and Gas Producer by 2020

However, although no one talks about it, America has a very, very serious and debilitating health problem, which is not an outbreak of "pleasantly plump," but true "obesity," which will inevitably change the demographic equation and at the same time blow apart future entitlement calculations. We are the fattest, most overweight country in the world, and as a result, our Medicare liabilities may be far bigger than anyone has predicted, an enormous burden perhaps crippling economic growth. I worry that this liability maybe could subtract at least a couple of PE multiple points from the future valuation of American equities.

About 35% of the U.S. population is technically obese, and for unexplained reasons in the last decade the percentage is rising at an accelerating pace. More Americans are becoming fat younger, and as a result diabetes, heart disease, and high blood pressure–related ailments are reaching epidemic proportions. A recent *New York Times* article pointed out that life expectancy around 1980 in many low-income, presumably less educated sections of the country where junk food consumption was high, was around 60 years, whereas it was close to 78 to 80 in the richer, educated areas. It attributed most of this discrepancy to unhealthy eating habits and consumption of sugary soft drinks. This combination and too little exercise was leading to a stunning rise in obesity, diabetes, high blood pressure, and depression related to the obesity.

A more recent study indicated that even though people in the poorer areas are becoming afflicted with diabetes and heart disease at younger ages, now their life expectancy has risen to 66 years of age. There was very little change in the health or longevity statistics of the wealthier. The improvements in the life expectancy of the lower classes is attributed to the development and broad usage of cholesterol-lowering statins such as Lipitor and advances in heart bypass surgery. The rate of cholesterol and high blood pressure in the obese has fallen dramatically in the last 20 years. The human body and its joints were designed to propel hunters and their lean families, not overweight, sedentary people. The resulting obesity has resulted in a huge increase in the number of hip and knee replacements, both of which are complicated and disabling procedures.

A paper in the August issue of *Health Affairs* states: "Obesity is being acquired at such young ages that you wonder what the limits of these technologies will be." Thus some other public health academics argue that our obesity trends threaten life expectancy and population growth because the advent of obesity at young ages may bring on other ailments such as kidney failures in later life. Another maintains rising obesity inevitably will lead to much higher levels of disability and medical care, which seems more likely to me based on what I saw last summer.

What these studies suggest to me is that more and more Americans are getting fatter younger, but that because of medical advances, the life expectancy of the lower, less educated groups probably is going to keep on rising. There is going to be a huge underclass of overweight people who will be partially disabled, lethargic, and suffering from a loss of self-esteem, and who are going to require a lot of expensive medical attention. James Vaupel, director of Duke University's Population Research Institute, emphasizes the disability factor. Other public health experts focus on the prospect of declining life expectancy. In other words, take your choice. America is either going to experience declining life expectancy and a falling population or continued population growth, but with much of it coming from disabled people.

I experienced the obesity epidemic firsthand last summer. Thanks to a lifetime of soccer, rugby, singles tennis on hard courts, and mountain climbing (and not because I was fat), I had to have a hip replacement. Incidentally my surgeon says it's coming down mountains and squash that do the most damage to your hips. Anyway, three days after the operation I went to an "acute rehabilitation" hospital for a week. It was one of the three worst weeks of my life. Right up there with the first weeks of the USMC platoon leaders' course and the first days of boarding school.

The rehab hospital was populated with 300 other patients recovering from knee and hip replacements. We were all forced to go from one place to another in wheelchairs. The other patients were almost all between 40 and 70 years old, and for the vast majority it was not sport or exercise that had caused their hips, knees, and in some cases backs to give out. They simply had eaten poorly and presumably too much and had exercised too little. The sad thing was that after the successful replacement surgery they were having terrible trouble rehabbing and regaining mobility because they were so overweight. Furthermore, they were prospects for further replacement surgery in the next 10 years because of their weight. This is not a minor problem. In 2012 there will be 550,000 hip replacement operations in the U.S. with the surgical, hospital, and rehab bills all one way or the other eventually paid for with taxpayer money. My surgical and rehab bill, 90% paid for by Medicare, was about $85,000 and that didn't include the primary or rehab hospital. Medicare sensibly will not pay for a single room, which I demanded after two days and nights in a double with a roomy with a hearing aid who endlessly watched TV game shows complete with canned laughter.

I know it's going to sound snotty, but I was also dismayed by how lethargic and indifferent to the rehab program many of the patients were. For hip replacements, the best rehab exercise of all is walking. Although there was an excellent outdoor circular track to walk on, practically no one did. It was also very disturbing to see that many of the older patients had just given up and were seemingly content to lie around all day watching TV. One of the side effects of obesity is depression and loss of self-esteem. I felt very sorry for them.

On the other hand, Americans have dramatically reduced cigarette and cigar smoking, which is a great accomplishment. Now another even more dangerous health tsunami appears to be bearing down on us from obesity. Smoking and lung cancer shortened lives, and as noted this new epidemic may or may not reduce life expectancy, but it will burden us with a ballooning, partially crippled and enfeebled population. Basically Americans are becoming a less healthy people. Real GDP growth is workforce growth plus productivity. Obesity threatens both and therefore real GDP growth. Japan here we come unless we forcefully deal with the threat. We are trying, but there are powerful commercial forces arrayed against progress. I am a phony since I own but do not consume McDonalds, Coke, Pepsi, et al. Incidentally fighting obesity is Mrs. Obama's prime cause!

2012

A Tough Call

"Prosperity ends in a crisis. The era of optimism dies in the crisis,
but in dying it gives birth to an era of pessimism. This new era is born,
not an infant, but a giant."

—*A.C. Pigou*

■ ■ ■

January 9, 2012

The high-frequency data from the U.S. continue to improve and to be above expectations. It's obviously very important that positive feedback loops are developing as consumer spending is reasonably healthy, employment is gradually rising, and as house prices seem to be stabilizing. Our contacts with corporate executives indicate volume and new orders are decent. Economists are saying the expansion is becoming self-sustaining, but I'm still concerned about the consumer's propensity to spend at these levels since it is not yet justified by growth in real incomes, and the savings rate is falling again.

It is also somewhat disconcerting that consumer debt to net worth ratios are still at 2008 levels because although debt has fallen, net worth has declined equally. That's not deleveraging. There could be a second half dip in the economy, but it looks as though 2012 will be a 2% real GDP year with corporate profits up slightly and the S&P 500 earnings per share around $105. The Bloomberg consensus is more optimistic and says the S&P is at 12 times this year's earnings and 8 times cash flow.

Meanwhile Europe including Germany is slipping and sliding into a deepening recession even as taxes are being increased and spending is being cut. Not exactly a Keynesian recipe. However, again Bloomberg's consensus still sees higher corporate profits for this year across Europe and if it is right European stocks are truly cheap selling at book value and 8.6 times earnings, 4 times cash flow, and yielding 5.5%. Even if it is wrong and profits are going to be lower, valuations are attractive. Of course Euroland has serious viability issues.

Japan's economy once again is faltering and is still mired in stag-deflation. China seems to be engineering a successful soft landing and the recent PMIs were encouraging and also exceeded all estimates. In my ignorant opinion, most of the chatter about the size of the real estate bubble in China and the prospects of its bursting and the banks collapsing is equally ignorant. "Nobody knows nuthin'" about China, but I think I know that valuations are ridiculously low unless all of China's statistics are complete fraud.

My guess is that the rest of non-Japan Asia can generate average growth of around 5% this year as central banks reassured about infla-tion take their feet off the brakes, and remains the most attractive area in the world. The transition from export to domestic demand-driven growth continues. Price action last year was disappointing to say the least, although some markets such as Indonesia and Thailand held up pretty well. Asia is the premier investment opportunity in the world. Buy ETFs for China, Taiwan, Korea, and Indonesia.

However, the big issue hanging over economies and markets is: Have we suffered enough for our past and present sins or are we doomed by the inexorability of fate and the excesses of human nature to suffer through an extended Hell of Austerity, a Great Stagnation, and agonizing wealth destruction? In other words, does another gigantic, consuming crisis lie ahead that will cause a horrendous, extended new era of eco-nomic distress and wealth destruction. I wish I had a high conviction answer, but I don't. As an optimist my intuition is that the worst is over, but I have to admit there is a nontrivial chance of an economic and financial apocalypse in the year to come and a long spell of lean years. The history of the world back to ancient times is that long cycles of wealth creation running two to three generations are invariably followed by a generation of wealth destruction. The post–World War II era from the late 1940s until somewhere around 2000–2006 was the greatest cycle of wealth creation ever. Since then there has been some serious wealth destruction, but are the gods appeased?

The apocalypse I worry about goes something like this. In the months to come the Europeans don't get their act together, Greece has a dis-orderly default, the sick countries are unable to refinance their matur-ing debt, the Euro as we know it today disappears, and the disruption and banking freeze-up caused by these events disrupts world trade and severely deepens the recession already underway in Europe. All this results in a global, double-dip recession including America which continues to struggle pathetically with its own political and entitlements issues. The global malaise is aggravated by social discontent and a vicious circle of stagnation and wealth destruction reminiscent of the 1930s and 1970s develops. The OECD recently released a survey that showed inequality of income and wealth was 1% vs. 99%, not just in America but in Sweden, Finland, Germany, etc. Even China has its own version, which it concedes is 2% and 98%. In such a skewed and distressed global environment there will be no sympathy or succor for banks, CEOs, the rich, hedge fund managers, or for investors, for that matter. In a desperate grasp for revenues, governments will raise taxes on capital and wealth, and equity markets could test or even break the lows of early 2009 as a vicious cycle of wealth destruction unfolds.

I put the odds of this scenario at 25%. Many other serious investors think it's more like 50-50. In such a world you even have to worry about the safety of the custodian of your assets, and there are few safe havens (Treasury Directs, farmland, timberland, owning real businesses come to mind). Moreover, since inflation seems bound to rise as fiscal and monetary policy vainly responds with impotent liquidity and stimulus, high-quality fixed-income investments and Treasuries have plenty of risk attached. Note that Treasury inflation-protected securities (TIPS) have a negative yield of 80 basis points. You are paying the government to store your money. Also unfortunately farmland and timber have already been exploited. Owning pedestrian, operating businesses that produce low-cost essentials could be the best investment, as they were during the 1930s. Maybe we should all buy McDonald's franchises.

Now as we start a new campaign, I am convinced equities are as cheap versus Treasuries as they have been since the 1930s. As noted above, in this turbulent, dangerous world there are no safe havens and gold has price risk and no yield. All things considered, a diversified list of high-quality American multinationals yielding around 3.5% with dividends rising faster than inflation and matchless liquidity looks as good as anything. However, make no mistake, in an apocalypse their prices will decline 20% or more. We also still believe emerging markets, particularly the Asian ones, are also fine, although riskier, investments.

On balance I am wary and occasionally terrified because of the apocalypse risk, but in calmer moments I can get particularly bullish. The gloom and doom scenario we outlined above is well known, and allocations to equities in portfolios ranging from giant pension and sovereign wealth funds to hedge funds are at record lows. Progress in Europe, an easing of the entitlement stalemate in the U.S., signs of a renewal in the emerging markets, and a moderate economic recovery would change the mood quickly and could even ignite a stampede.

I enter the New Year with a moderate net long of about 60% and my concentrations remain in the U.S. (technology, oil service, energy, natural gas, and industrial manufacturing) and Asia (China, Hong Kong, Indonesia, Taiwan, Korea, Thailand). I'm mindful of the apocalypse risk but also to the potential for a 10% or 20% rally. There are a lot of very cheap stocks. In long-only accounts I hold 25% cash.

A.C. Pigou was a classmate of Keynes, and I meditate on his stunning utterance. What a dramatic conception. It was pointed out to me by the wise Edward Chancellor. A new, giant infant could be being conceived and about to be born. It would be very painful to miss this giant's childhood. Bear in mind it is the hard reality of investment life that it is almost impossible to have both cheap valuations on equities and good news. We currently have cheap valuations and bad news. Thus it is possible a substantial rally in risk assets could develop not because the news is good but simply because the news is less bad than what has already been discounted.

No Bull

In January, I travelled to Dubai to speak at a conference sponsored by a Saudi firm, The Family Office. They have a very systematic and rational approach to managing the affairs of wealthy Middle Eastern families and I was very impressed. The audience was mostly Arabs and it was sophisticated and responsive. It was my first visit to Dubai in seven years and I loved it.

They have done a beautiful job with the city, the roads, and the airport. The presentations at the conference were excellent. Gazing at night at a skyline in which a third of the elegant buildings are totally unoccupied is an enlightening experience.

■ ■ ■

January 26, 2012

No bull? Maybe a lot of bull! Anyway I was just in the Middle East and heard mucho from "reliable sources" (including two former area heads of MI 6 and the CIA) that was contrary to the conventional wisdom. Not completely sure what it all means but anyway here goes.

I was told that in Syria the insurrection is being underwritten, supported in a big way by the Gulf States and the Saudi Sunni establishment because they view Iran as their mortal enemy and the Assad regime as the creature of Iran. The regime in Syria is Alawite (an offshoot of Shi'a Islam) and is a destabilizing force in the Middle East.

On the other hand, they say the backers of Assad are Israel and the far right Sunni Wahabi Arabs, an unholy alliance if there ever was one. Israel apparently prefers the devil it knows and can live with, Assad, to a new, revolutionary Syria. The hard-core far right Wahabis support Assad because Syria is the functioning pipeline for Hamas and other terrorist groups.

A little over a year ago on a visit to Damascus I spent some time with Bashir Assad and am mortified to confess I was disarmed and charmed by him and his deputy prime minister for economic affairs as they described their grand plans to normalize relations with the U.S. and to jump-start growth in Syria by building toll roads, dams, power stations, etc. We talked with the deputy prime minister about private equity investments in these projects and a sovereign debt issue for the country. Assad seemed a gentle, compassionate man hurled by fate (his older brother crashed his sports car) and family into a role he didn't relish. I have asked myself repeatedly how I could have been so wrong!

However, last week I was told by someone who over the years had numerous contacts with Assad that the regime really did want to elevate the standard of living of the Syrian people. They wanted, needed to provide progress so they could remain in power. However, that doesn't mean that if you are utterly committed to creating an enduring family dynasty, as the Assads are, that you can tolerate dissent. You have to be prepared to ruthlessly destroy anyone and everyone who opposes you or calls for an open society. Assad's father, when confronted with rebellion 30 years ago, squashed it by literally leveling a revolutionary city and murdering an estimated 20,000. Undoubtedly, the source said, the Assads remember that although the massacre caused much hand wringing in the U.N., there was no intervention and the regime survived and prospered. Now they probably think that when confronted with the Arab Spring, the other Middle East dictators weren't tough enough and rolled over too easily. The Assad family has no intention of making the same mistake. Moreover, the fates of Gadaffi and Mubarak must be very sobering. Incidentally, I also heard talk of a Kuwaiti Spring and that Bahrain remains a tender flashpoint.

So this brings up the subject of Saudi Arabia. The monarchy is a complex situation and the Saudi businesspeople I talked with are very concerned that instability could be occurring in the royal family at a time of extreme turmoil in the Arab world. The elite, nonroyal Saudis say that the monarchy is entrenched and well respected. However, succession is the problem, and a recent assassination attempt almost succeeded, a security failure that shocked the Saudi establishment because King Abdullah is so carefully protected. The story is that an important Yemen sheik, whose tribe had long been an enemy, told the Saudis he and his people were ready to make peace. The Saudis were thrilled. Then the sheik said it was required that he personally must hand his ceremonial scimitar to the king himself to make it clear to his people he really was surrendering. I gather somewhat reluctantly the Saudis agreed because it is policy never to risk the king's person.

On the day of the ceremony the sheik must have been searched and patted down before entering the throne room, but he had stuffed enough explosives up his anus to blow up himself and the king, and he planned to detonate as he delivered the sword. Talk about "intestinal fortitude"! Something went wrong in the throne room, perhaps some unexpected flatulence, and he suddenly exploded 15 yards from the king, killing himself and several courtiers, but not injuring the King. The source said, "They scraped the sheik off the ceiling." Scary stuff! Cannot find any reference to this episode on Google but the source is unimpeachable.

King Abdullah himself is 85, has a very bad back, and is being treated for cancer. The crown prince is also in his 80s and infirm, and there are no rules for the clear line of succession after the death of the current crown prince except that future rulers have to be direct ancestors of the founder of the modern Saudi Arabia, King Abdel al Aziz. The next king should come from a generation in which there are believed to be about 100 grandsons, many of whom would like to be king and some of whom apparently have pushy wives who would like them to be king. My informant said that although these women have no official standing and still aren't allowed to drive, they have considerable influence.

Essentially "the royal family" decides, although a recently created family council of the sons and grandsons of King Aziz that has 35 members may be the ultimate arbiter. I have been reading Robert Massie's new biography of Catherine the Great, which is fascinating but ponderous (800 pages). It describes in somewhat overwhelming detail the intrigues and convolutions of the Russian court as the descendants of Peter the Great schemed for the crown before Catherine came to power. There were nowhere near as many protagonists in that weird drama as there are in the Saudi royal family power struggles, which I am told are now going on. My guess is that 10 years, 20 years from now there will be five kings in the world—the king of England and the four in the deck of cards.

The other surprising revelation was that the U.S. fifth fleet in the gulf and its precious aircraft carriers may not be as invulnerable as is thought. The Iranian admiral's warnings and threats should not be totally disregarded as ridiculous blustering bellicosity. In the event of closing the Straits of Hormuz, not only does Iran have plans to lay 700 mines, a U.S. navy study notes that the Iranians have been developing the capability to "swarm" the U.S. fleet with "possibly more than one thousand" small, souped-up speedboats loaded with explosives and driven by one or two men from the Revolutionary Guard Navy Corps committed to suicide. Such an unconventional, low-tech attack would be hard to detect and deal with even with the fleet's sophisticated electronic countermeasures, and if just three or four boats could penetrate the screen and ram a carrier or cruiser, they could disable or sink a capital ship.

In addition, the Iranians would simultaneously launch a large number of cruise missiles. The U.S. navy's massive air superiority would be ineffective against this kind of threat, and apparently there is concern that even its very sophisticated fire control systems would be overwhelmed by over 1,000 sea and air targets. A study from MIT ominously states: "The U.S. fleet defenses have never been tested in combat against an adversary with a large number of cruise missiles." The chances of capital ships being damaged or other ships being sunk are not minimal. This onslaught is being called "swarming," a unique tactic that Iran close to its home bases in a restricted seaway could unleash. Remember that the Iranians used "human waves" effectively against the Iraqis in the Iran-Iraq war, and that they attacked 550 oil tankers passing through the Straits of Hormuz during the so-called "Tanker War" 25 years ago. During that skirmish after a U.S. frigate was badly damaged, the U.S. retaliation, Operation Praying Mantis, seriously bloodied the Iranian navy and oil infrastructure.

As far as Israel is concerned, a very wise and sophisticated Jewish friend says that the Arabs should realize that left to itself Israel will explode. His point is that the conservative, orthodox Jews in Israel are totally out of control and are fracturing the country's social and body politic, antagonizing Israel's foreign friends, and could be even destroying the state with their extremist positions.

What does all this mean except that the Middle East is truly an inscrutable, complex mess? Maybe nothing new of investment significance. Mr. Market already knows the Middle East has been and is a dangerous place, and that something bad could happen that would disrupt oil flows through the straits, causing a big price spike in crude, which would be very tough for the world economy. Mr. Market knows all this but would nevertheless be appalled if it happened.

Finally a word about Dubai, which is really a city, not a country. If you haven't been there, you should. Fifteen years ago Dubai was a small desert sheikdom of 400,000 people with no oil, where they fished, dived for pearls, and bred camels. Then from the ruling family, the al-Maktoums, came a sheik with imagination and guts who conceived of a modern, sophisticated, adult Disneyland with no behavior restraints on dress or drinking that would attract Arabs and also Western tourists. The rumor is that there is also a horde of whores, but if so I didn't see any. The al-Maktoums also created "knowledge villages," "silicon centers," and a sophisticated financial center. The Dubai skyline is the most spectacular in the world, dominated by a 130-story, minaret-thin office building, but don't misunderstand—the spectacle is architecturally inspiring and in good taste.

Dubai is six or seven hours by air from cold and rainy Europe and the climate is a sure thing. Of course it's very hot in the summer, but when I was just there the weather was ideal. Temperature ranges from 65 at night to 80 midday, dry, blue sky, sun all day long, and wonderful Red Sea swimming. Every diversion from "dead, solid, perfect golf" to first-class restaurants, great street atmosphere, night life, and even indoor skiing. The highway system works magnificently, and the nearby superb airport is served by Emirates—the best airline in the world. People are friendly and welcoming. Totally safe. Like Monaco, rowdy, obnoxious behavior is not tolerated, and the bad guys get arrested and thrown in the slammer. Then the authorities conveniently lose the key for 30 days. Not a destination for rowdy college kids.

The other fascination for those of us studying booms and busts in a bubble-prone world is the real estate cycle in Dubai. In the 2000s as Dubai vaulted onto the world stage and as both Arabs and Europeans flocked, there was massive construction, both commercial and residential. For example, in a few years the price of a two-bedroom apartment with an ocean view soared from $300,000 to $2 million. Every jackass developer and bank in the world got involved, and a building boom of mind-boggling proportions developed. Today, roughly a third of that jagged, fantastic skyline is artistic, but half-finished buildings and the price of that two bedroom has plummeted to around $250,000 to $275,000. Construction has stopped and a million guest workers have been sent home. Dubai World, the emir's state-owned holding company accumulated $80 billion of debt. For a moment a few years ago the country and the sheikdom itself looked like it was bust, but then Dubai's next-door cousin, Abu Dhabi, which does have enormous oil reserves (and a real estate bust of its own), bailed out the government at least for the time being.

It seems the non–real estate and construction sector, which is 75% of the Dubai economy, is doing fine. Hotel occupancies are high, shopping malls filled, squares busy with people, Starbucks everywhere, restaurant reservations difficult, and the new financial center humming. However, it's going to take years, maybe a decade, to work off the most gigantic, highly visible real estate inventory imaginable. It's fascinating to see, and the excesses must have been so obvious, yet the money kept being lent and construction kept going. On the Grantham Mayo web site there is a magnificent piece by Edward Chancellor about the anatomy of extreme real estate cycles, but I don't think even Chicago 100 years ago was as obvious as this one.

If you're adventurous, the Dubai sovereigns two-year sovereign debt yields 5.27%, the 10-year is a little over 7%. Dubai Holdings' 10-year maturities yields are around 12%.

I'm still 65% net long. Terrified of missing what could be a powerful extension of the rally if the global economy continues to recover and scared to death that real reform is still not occurring in Europe and that there continues to be a meaningful risk of a euro apocalypse and a double-dip recession. I still put the odds of the latter outcome at 25%.

The Elderly Kid Goes to a Tech Conference

February 23, 2012

Last week I attended a technology and Internet conference in San Francisco put on by a famous investment banking firm. Why did I go? Because I'm a dilettante in tech, although I have a big position in the sector and hoped—expected—to learn something. What I learned is that I'm not just a dilettante; I'm a hopeless, ignorant dilettante. Decorative but insignificant! Unfortunately, there were no moments of rare and precious content.

Also, I was anxious to take the temperature of the new tech crowd and the milieu it swims in. Had they studied the carcasses of the likes of Wang, Digital Equipment, and Nortel and learned anything? Did they know that the history of the high-growth span of even the great tech companies was 4.5 years or about the same as that of an NFL running back? Finally, I wanted to see the powerful and gifted corporate rainmakers up front, close, and personal; at least that was my illusion. Up close and personal? There were over 1,000 analysts and investors at this conference even though there's another major tech gathering in three weeks.

The demography and mood of the tech crowd is important to me. Their interpretations and pronouncements dominate the action. My impression was that they're true believers. They're young, skinny, and all seem to have large, grape-shaped heads perched on long necks. They sit all day expressionless, fiercely concentrating, clutching their laptops or iPads, eyes focused on the screens, tapping relentlessly at their keyboards, presumably transcribing the incomprehensible complexities of the presentations. They don't seem to interact or talk much to each other, although occasionally they mumble something to themselves. It's like being with a bunch of silent, somewhat geeky giraffes.

Here's the meeting format. The conference runs three days. All meetings are Charlie Rose–style "fireside chats." The CEO or CFO being

185

interviewed sits at a small table on the stage and is questioned by the analyst that covers the company. Each day there were two high-profile, 45-minute, "Keynote" firesides in the mammoth ballroom commencing at 8:00 in the morning, and then at 12:30 two more over gross, austerity box lunches that you tasted all afternoon. In between, six different tracks of 40-minute firesides are taking place with lesser companies. The last session ends at about 6:00 in the evening, and by then 48 companies have been firesided. In addition, all day there are smaller "breakout" sessions for those that want to ask specific questions of a management, and in the evening there are company dinners. It's very intense. The giraffes transform into a herd, hugging their desktops and iPads, eyes glazed, and silently race frantically from one venue to another with occasional desperate stampedes to a really hot company presentation.

At the conference, about half the time I didn't understand what was being said, although I now know what the "distributive cloud" is and what VMware does. It "takes the complexity out of infrastructure." Helpful, huh? However, statements such as "it's a tornado market," "we are thread optimized," and "the cloud foundry is beta right now" didn't tell me anything, although everyone else seemed intent on transcribing them onto their iPads. I guess I can figure out what "virtualizing the installed estate" and "unearthing patterns to enhance analysis" means. They must have a course in creative tech speak at MIT and Caltech because every company's "footprint is robust," they were "early adopters," other people's markets all are "bloody," and no one has "sun-setting products." Bundling, big data mining, enabling technologies, and microarchitecture and the consumerization of computer use also were phrases heard frequently.

In terms of the current business environment, the tone at the conference was positive—U.S. better, Europe a little soft, Asia strong but lumpy. The consumer is reviving and most companies seem to think the second half of this year will be better than the first, but they are not anticipating a surging economy like 2009. Inventories everywhere are lean. As companies generate cash flow, acquisitions of new technologies with stock or cash have become attractive versus internal R&D, where the eventual output is uncertain because with the former at least you know what you are going to get. There is also a favorable accounting impact.

I think I heard five themes. First, that, yes, all hot tech products eventually become commodities but it happens slower than the conventional wisdom thinks, so that the "first movers" usually have 8 to 10 years of prosperity. Second, that the pace of productivity change continues to be rapid. For example, 5G phones with 5G Wi-Fi will have three times the performance, twice the range, use less power, and will be half the price. Third, there is a lot of demand for a better, longer-lasting battery. Fourth, creating or enhancing an international brand presence for a product is very expensive and absolutely essential. Fifth, Texas Instruments and several other companies said cell phones are still a dynamic but highly competitive market. They are not yet a commodity, and front-end access to the cloud is coming, whatever that means. Finally, migration to the cloud is one of the biggest shifts in tech history, and cloud computing will grow sixfold to over $240 billion by 2020.

The much anticipated fireside with Tim Cook, who now runs Apple, was fascinating as it was his first public appearance with the crowd. He even looks a little like Steve Jobs—lean, esthetic, articulate, quite passionate. The analyst interviewing him initially served up a softball that must have been prearranged about Apple's manufacturing practices in Asia, which Cook answered with a long, boring, self-righteous diatribe. Then it got more interesting. "Everyone in the world is looking for the best product," Cook said. "Not the cheapest version of the best product." He went on. The iPad has a trajectory like nothing else, and Apple is still trying and experimenting with Apple TV, but he suggested gently that he didn't necessarily think it had huge potential. The iPhone and the iPad, as they mature, will become royalty plays as Apple gets its share of new features. He also answered evasively, but well, the question of what they were going to do about the $100 billion in cash, saying they were "deliberately" thinking about it. I think a substantial regular dividend is the most likely outcome.

Cook projected real charisma. The other CEOs of the big, successful tech companies came across as intelligent, diligent engineers but I didn't see much evidence of the vision thing. No zip to their remarks; occasional verbal infelicities. However, they have a tough job. It must be incredibly difficult to forecast the level of acceptance and demand for a new chip or flash memory device, but nevertheless you have to make your bet on the manufacturing plant. If you don't build enough capacity you may be caught short if your new, new thing is a "tornado" but on the other hand endure a big financial hit if it's a dud.

So is the tech ecosystem fevered? The first chart shows that the NDX broad tech index is still far below its epic bubble high of almost 400 at the end of March 2000. Technically speaking, it has broken through its May 2011 recovery high, but breadth and the number of weekly new highs is diminishing. Is the Facebook IPO going to be the top? Exhaustion?

The second chart, courtesy of Doug Kass, shows that for the last 10 years the NDX has gradually, inexorably outperformed the S&P 500. Facebook, the private company investment boom, the conference, the fact that tech is the most popular sector for institutional investors, and the current Internet IPO boom are worrying some astute investors. I disagree. I think the rush has further to go. Sure there is madness in the Internet, social networking, start-up world, but valuations of the vast majority of big-capitalization tech are reasonable and a fresh capital spending cycle seems to be underway.

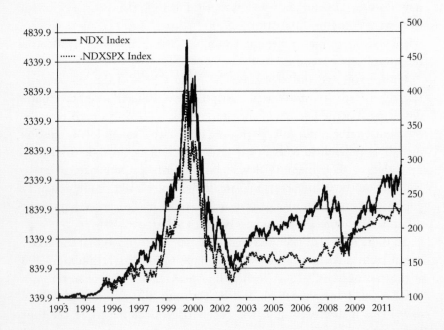

Valuations of the more mature, big "old" tech companies such as Cisco, Intel, IBM, and Microsoft are low to mid-teens on forward earnings. These are cyclical growth companies with broad product exposure capable of growing earnings faster than the S&P 500, but are no longer the dynamic boomers they once were. Why shouldn't they sell at a premium multiple to the S&P? With tech spending on the rise, they look like good investments.

The new tech superstars such as Apple, Amazon, Google, Qualcomm, Broadcom, EMC, Juniper, et al. are valued in the high and low 20s on expected earnings but have the potential to bang out 15% to 20% earnings gains for the next few years. Of course there are exceptions, like VMware blissfully floating in the cloud, and Amazon that are at altitude, but then you have Apple ex-cash at less than 10 times. The small-cap tech world is not particularly crazy. The semiconductor stocks may already be beginning to roll over. To me it doesn't seem like the *Hindenburg* yet.

Positive Change at the Margin Continues

I was up 13% for the year to date on this date. It wouldn't last. The U.S. economy and corporate earnings were looking good, but Greece and Europe would rear their ugly head again.

■ ■ ■

March 16, 2012

*H*ere we are with equity markets hovering around recovery highs and threatening to break out. Nevertheless, the world is still a mess with an ugly bunch of structural problems, although perhaps a little less messy than a few months ago. What to do now? My reaction is that it's too soon to take off risk and that at the margin the chances of a financial apocalypse and a double-dip recession with all of its drastic social consequences have diminished quite significantly. There is still a huge amount of hedge fund and long-only money that has missed this rally and is hurting.

To be specific, the threat of a euro-European breakup has lessened; a slow, gradual economic recovery seems to be taking hold in the U.S., China, and most other parts of the world; and a war with Iran skyrocketing the price of oil appears less likely. Are we for sure out of the dark, deep woods? No, of course not, but maybe after a long, five-year stretch of more and more bad stuff happening, we are going to get an interlude of better weather. If so, equities will be the primary beneficiary as investors scramble out of their dimly lit, minimal-return storm cellars into the sunlight. What is the evidence of this improvement at the margin?

First of all, Europe seems to have avoided a disorderly Greek debt default, and with the ECB leading the way, the outlines of firewalls and a three-year recovery program are emerging. Is it nothing but kicking the proverbial can three years down the road? Perhaps, but it will buy time for fiscal discipline to be restored. Progress towards reform in Italy without riots and broken windows is encouraging, and Italian interest rates and spreads have fallen. Of course the process is still extremely fragile, but there are baby steps in the right direction. The odds of an apocalypse, a breakup of the euro, and a financial crisis that would rock the world have receded. However, Europe has not solved its solvency problem and precious time has been bought, but Europe's future will depend on whether the interlude is used or abused.

Second, global economic growth momentum is building even as the global central bank easing cycle continues. The J.P. Morgan global PMI rose to a 12-month high of 55.5% in February, and the indications this week are that this trend is continuing and, just maybe, a virtuous circle is developing. The U.S. economy continues to surprise with encouraging employment data, a four-year low in unemployment claims, a non-manufacturing PMI of 57.3%, big gains in vehicle production and sales, a homebuilders survey at a six-year high, and rising consumer and executive confidence. A dozen swallows don't make a spring but they aren't a sign of winter either.

Meanwhile, the second biggest economy in the world, China, also seems to have successfully engineered a soft landing and with inflation falling, rate cuts could be coming. Of course, the China bears are screaming that it's all a fraud and an illusion, but there is a touch of desperation in their shrillness. Three other big economies in Asia, Taiwan, Indonesia, and Korea, are picking up, and wonder of all wonders, Japan, number three in the world, is showing some signs of life. The bull story there is that the Bank of Japan finally, at long last, got it and understands it has to buy bonds and print money. Note that the Fed apparently is considering a "sterilized" QE3. Bernanke apparently has decided, with a fiscal cliff looming at the end of the year, that the consequences of a double dip are so dangerous that he is not going to take any chances on an abort. Now, global short rates are falling again.

Third, the odds of a conflagration in the Middle East have diminished. The U.S. has clearly and quite artfully signaled Israel and its prime minister that we do not believe Iran currently is building a nuclear weapons capability, and that we are not on for a joint attack. Furthermore, I am told by "reliable sources" that the elite New York Jewish community is not in favor of an Israeli air strike at this time either, nor is the Israeli middle class or military establishment. The threat of an attack and war with Iran has already pushed up the price of oil, and in the event of an attack would send it soaring to crippling levels and almost certainly would bring on a global double dip. In the last six weeks, the Iran and the price-of-oil risk has plagued markets. It would be very helpful if oil prices now declined $15 or $20 a barrel.

I haven't changed my portfolio much. I'm 80% net long. Heavy America and Asia. U.S. technology, China–Hong Kong, and Italian stocks are still my biggest positions. I have added Japanese equities with a hedge short of the yen and some Russia. My short in the U.S. 10-year Treasury bond has worked out well, but I wish I had done more. I'm not inclined to add with the yield at 2.28%. However, a rally back to 2% would be appealing. "Don't fight the Fed." If the central bank prints massive amounts of paper, eventually inflation will rise. The 10-year U.S. Treasury currently has an inflation-adjusted negative yield of around 80 to 100 basis points. Could the 10-year be yielding close to 5% three years from now with nominal GDP 5% (3% inflation + 2% real GDP)? I think so. Treasuries at current prices truly are "Certificates of Confiscation" as Lee Cooperman calls them. However, if I were in Bernanke's position, I would be doing what he is doing—printing money. Of course, there will be distortions created by quantitative easing, such as penalizing saving and promoting consumption at a time when the savings rate is already too low, but the consequences of an Austrian-style double dip would be far worse.

What could go wrong? The negatives are the aforementioned rise in oil and gasoline prices and also that a fiscal cliff in the U.S. looms at the end of the year. Bank loans in the U.S. have rolled over, and bank stocks have been weak in Europe. Corporate profit margins in the U.S. and elsewhere seem to have peaked as labor costs rise and productivity gains slow. The January U.S. trade deficit will knock slightly less than 1% off first-quarter real GDP, and the S&P 500 now appears to be earning a $95-a-share annual rate. Equities are only truly cheap versus interest rates, not in absolute terms.

On the other hand, Doug Kass points out that risk premiums (earnings yield less than the risk-free cost of capital) are back up to 1974 levels and that the S&P 500 in 1975 soared 32% and another 19% in 1976. Stocks peaked in 1966 and the great, crushing secular bear market that began in 1966 bottomed in 1974, but then the new, secular bull market didn't really begin until six years later in 1982. Similar patterns have been traced out in most of the major market secular swings of modern times.

This time, in aggregate, the return on equities has been negative since the late 1990s, but the main U.S. and European indexes have already rallied over 20% since the October lows, so if this is the 1974 cycle all over again, we have already had two-thirds of the 1975 fun. Hedge funds actually reduced their net long positions last week and pension funds and endowments are at generational lows in equities. I think the pain trade is still up.

Simpson Bowles Forever

April 11, 2012

*G*etting a "grand bargain" is crucial for America. We are lucky to have patriots like Alan Simpson and Chester Bowles. Depressing that they think another financial crisis is necessary to bring the American people, the special interest groups, and the politicians to the point of compromise.

A lethal, poisonous uncertainty hanging over U.S. markets (and world markets for that matter) is the so-called Fiscal Cliff. As of January 1, 2013, the Bush tax cuts, the temporary payroll tax cut, and long-term unemployment benefits will all expire. To make matters worse, on January 15, because of the failure of the Joint Select Committee on Deficit Reduction, other formulaic draconian cuts will go into effect, which in total will abruptly subtract about 350 basis points of real GDP from what will still be a fragile economy expanding at perhaps 2%. This is the Fiscal Cliff the economy faces.

Unfortunately, there's another precipice looming—a Monetary Cliff that is even steeper and more hazardous. By the fall of this year, it will become very evident that the U.S. is living beyond its means and that there is an entitlements deficit of truly mountainous proportions. By December of this year, we will be bumping up against the national debt ceiling and a possible downgrade of our sovereign debt. The budget and the deficit are out of control. Just as serious is the enormous liability America has created in the last 10 years of unfunded promises to pay to our people when they retire and for their medical expenses. Investors, businessmen, and the people themselves sense these lethal imbalances, and if they are not addressed, they eventually will erode confidence, consumer and capital spending, and will drastically affect valuations. This is the Entitlements Cancer.

In my opinion, although the Monetary Cliff is more long-term dangerous, the proximity of the Fiscal Cliff, if not dealt with, will trigger the dreaded double-dip recession we are all terrified of and bring on another financial crisis. Congress could deal with this issue over the course of this year, but is that a realistic hope with a cantankerous, highly partisan Congress while an election is going on? Is a Lame Duck Congress likely to get anything done (supposing Obama is reelected and the House and Senate are Republican)? Of course, the other alternative is that Congress defers the issue, in effect kicking the can down the road again, but the tolerance of the equity and fixed-income vigilantes has been stretched thin. And make no mistake; the vigilantes are international, cold-blooded, and very powerful, and they are like wolves attacking a weak and wounded buffalo.

The debt extension is no minor event. Here are some nasty facts. The average maturity of the U.S. Treasury debt is five years, and the average interest rate is 2.2%, so the interest expense last year was about $450 billion. Since inflation is running close to 3%, in total, the owners of Treasuries have a negative real return. About 70% of the total—or $5.9 trillion—is the amount of debt coming due in the next five years. Unless an economic miracle occurs, additional Treasuries will have to be sold in the years to come to fund the budget deficit. This year, according to Bloomberg Economics columnist Caroline Baum, a 100-basis-point increase in the average interest rate will add $88 billion of interest expense. Last year, the Federal Reserve bought 61% of the new debt issuance and foreigners (probably most of the central banks, particularly of China) purchased about 20%.

Thus we are very dependent on the Fed and the kindness of strangers for the rollover of our national debt. One of those strangers, China, is already choking on T-bonds and has expressed its reluctance to increase its holdings. Japan is transitioning to its own quantitative easing. Suppose China and Japan not only stopped buying but actually tried to sell. Baum puts it succinctly: "The U.S. is more dependent on short-term funding than many of Europe's most indebted countries, including Greece and Spain."

I recently attended a breakfast with former Senator Alan Simpson, Erskine Bowles, and Mayor Bloomberg. I think the Simpson Bowles Committee (SBC), appointed by the president (which incidentally was truly bipartisan), came up with reasonable compromise solutions to these big issues, but which do require a pound of flesh from everyone.

Subsequently, the president and the majority leader dropped it like a hot potato. Everyone got fat in the last 10 to 15 years and now Mr. Everyone is going to have to lose some weight. Since we are an equal society, the top echelons are going to have to give up the most. A few weeks ago, the SBC was summarily dismissed by the House. We are a nation of totally self-centered special interest groups that terrorize our politicians. Our politicians are scared to death of them. As Senator Simpson, a life-long Republican and one-time minority leader of the Senate, put it, "If President Obama had endorsed our proposals, they would have torn him limb from limb."

The "they" whom he was talking about principally is the American Association of Retired People (AARP), which has 45 million members and is growing by 10,000 new members a day. The AARP is a single-issue voting bloc, and on election day it can turn out its members, most of whom have not much else to do. Social Security is their bête noire. In the late 1930s, when FDR created Social Security, the average life expectancy of Americans was around 60 and there were 33 workers for every beneficiary. The retirement age was set at 65 and benefits were later indexed to inflation. Today, the life expectancy is close to 80 and there are 3 workers on the way to 2 for each beneficiary. The retirement age is still 65. The Social Security System is bankrupt with an unfunded liability in the trillions that is rising every day. The SBC recommended that the retirement age be gradually raised over 20 years to 70, and that the Social Security payroll tax assessment be raised from the first $110,000 to $175,000. Of course, the *other* AARP (the American Association of Rich People) screamed bloody murder as they do about any tax rate increase on higher-income payers.

The same dynamics apply to Medicare, and here the SBC suggested maintaining the Medicare cost controls associated with the recent health-care reform legislation and increasing the authority of the Independent Payment Advisory Board. Again, the AARP went nuts, screaming about "death panels." The issue is that at a huge expense, modern medicine can prolong hopelessly dying people's lives until they are virtually vegetables. End-of-life care is a major reason health insurance is insolvent.

The SBC also proposed a $200 billion reduction in discretionary spending with proposed cuts including reducing defense procurement by 15%, closing one third of overseas bases, eliminating "earmarks," and cutting the federal workforce by 10%. In addition, it suggested $100 billion in increased tax revenues through reforms such as introducing a 15%

gasoline tax and eliminating or restricting a number of exemptions, such as the home mortgage interest deduction on expensive homes and the deduction for employer-provided healthcare benefits. Another proposal was a reduction in entitlements including farm subsidies, federal pension service reform, and student loan subsidies. Senator Simpson points out that last year we spent $740 billion on defense; the next 14 biggest spending countries combined spent $560 billion.

The tax reform proposed by the SBC is staggering in its dimensions. Almost all deductions are eliminated, capital gains and dividends are taxed as income, and we go to three brackets (12%, 20%, and 27%). All corporate and individual deductions and exemptions including mortgages, earmarks, and charitable contributions are gone, as is the alternative minimum tax. A federal excise tax on gasoline goes into effect in 2015. However, all this is another, very complex subject. All manner of fiscal experts have objected, showing disastrous consequences. Senator Simpson just smiles: "Torture statistics long enough and they will confess to anything."

Alan Simpson and Erskine Bowles are great Americans and their program needs serious consideration. At the breakfast, Bowles said he had just spent time with the president and that Obama had told him after the election he thought progress would occur. Someone then asked Simpson, Bowles, and Bloomberg whether they thought these issues could be dealt with without another financial crisis occurring first. All three regretfully said they did NOT think so. Depressing!

As for the markets short term, my guess is that we are about halfway through a correction slash pullback, whatever. The U.S. market for the next month will be data and European dependent. The American economy is looking a little soggy here, but I think the 2% momentum is still up. Europe seems stuck again. That the ECB and EFSF are already talking about spending their precious firewall funds that are supposed to last for three years is not cheery. Italy today sold one-year paper at 2.84%, whereas a month ago it financed at 1.40%. Germany's financing stumbled, too. It's clear Europe is in a recession that is affecting everyone, including former stalwarts like the Netherlands. I'm out of Italy and have sold short some French and German equities.

Shake Well Before Using

Early May 2012

t seems to me eventually Greece is going to have to leave the euro. Equity markets are still of the view that an exit would be disorderly and catastrophic for the rest of the euro bloc, the world economy, and equity markets. I'm inclined to disagree. I think a Greek exit, if handled properly and if the European authorities stand their ground and make absolutely clear that they will employ their firewall funds to effectively defend Spain, Italy, and Portugal, would be bullish for other equity markets around the world that are currently being pummeled. The other European countries have their ailments, but Greece has a malignant cancer that needs surgery and radiation.

The recent Greek elections showed that the "Greek street" has had all the austerity it will accept. By some measures, Greece has had a depression of deeper magnitude than the U.S. experienced in the 1930s. Now, the newly empowered political parties are refusing to honor the terms of the country's international loan agreements. Chaos reigns! Within the euro bloc, Greece has years of even deeper pain ahead. Greece desperately needs its own currency and a major devaluation to restore its competiveness and to begin curing its ills. A devaluation (surgery) would cause massive "creative destruction" in Greece but buy the time to implement the reforms that are so essential.

The Greeks seem to be relying on the rest of Europe to come up with the funds to kick the Greek can down the road one more time. They hope the fear of contamination and the commitment to sustaining the euro is so powerful that the rest of Europe will continue to prop them up. Certainly the Germans and the European elite want to preserve the euro for both economic and political reasons, but Europe is not ready to become the United States of Europe with all the commonality that it implies.

Meanwhile, the Germans are getting tougher. A few days ago, the German Finance Minister Wolfgang Schaeuble stated that membership in the European Union is voluntary and Greece has a choice. The press reports the German people are predominantly of the opinion that they do not want to provide further support to the "shiftless, deceitful, and self-indulgent" Greeks, and that they and the rest of Europe would be better off with Greece out of the Eurozone.

The powers that be in Europe, principally Germany and almost certainly the IMF, are adamant that Greece must fulfill its treaty commitments or there will be no more transfusions of money. I don't blame them. The Greeks lied about their finances in order to get into the Euro, and subsequent governments have failed to take most of the measures, from tax collecting to labor reforms that were so obviously essential, to improve the country's financial position. Now they have to endure the consequences.

The fear that pervades markets today is that an exit from the euro by Greece would vastly intensify the financial contamination that is already being created. Presently, the vigilantes are attacking other troubled European countries' financial instruments, and stock markets are falling, credit spreads are widening, and sovereign debt rates are climbing. At this moment, Spain, Italy, and Portugal are the three principal targets. Tomorrow, who knows? A total breakup of the euro and a shutdown of the global banking system (albeit temporary) would be a catastrophe for the world economy and would almost certainly engender the feared double dip. Longer term, the issue of whether the Eurozone and its currency can survive in a bloc of divergent countries without a common fiscal policy remains to be seen.

My partner Amer Bisat, who spent 10 years at the IMF, tells me he thinks the European authorities are not yet prepared for such adventurous action. The memory of 2008–2009 haunts them and they worry that Greece could be Europe's Lehman with similar profound, catastrophic consequences for markets and the global economy. He argues the ECB does not yet have its full firewall funds in place, and that with an exit, the speculators would smell blood and would savage Spanish and Italian paper. The powers that be are more likely to try to buy time by giving Greece some more money now in the hope that nine months or a year from now, reforms and recovery will have built a healthier Europe.

If my rosy scenario works out, in which Greece is not thrown one more lifeline and told to go and if (a huge if) the other sickly countries are successfully defended, I think equity markets should resume their march higher. I think the U.S. and Asian markets would be the prime beneficiaries. Often wrong, never in doubt.

This Business Is Getting More Complicated

Could oil save us? Everyone is gloomy here as May fades into June. Europe is a mess and it is not apparent how the Old Continent extricates itself without triggering another financial panic. The European banking system can't live with the losses and disruption of Greece going out of the euro, but the resources and political will are not there to keep it in the euro. At the same time European economic data are getting weaker with Germany's manufacturing PMI plunging to 45.

Meanwhile the U.S. economy meanders along without much conviction, and China depending on whom you believe and your point of view remains the hope of the world or a disaster. As I point out in the following essay, "nobody knows nuthin'." What we do know is that investor sentiment everywhere is very bearish but not yet at the levels of February and March 2009. In America equity mutual funds outflows in the first four months of 2012 were a record and twice the same periods in 2008 and 2009. However, in the first two weeks of this May they were triple the average of the first four months! Aggressive long only managers and hedge funds continue to raise cash and reduce risk. My net long is down to about 50%. I recall with trepidation the old adage that the likelihood of a market decline is inversely proportional to the size of your cash position.

What follows is the general transcript of a real conversation modified as to his identity. What makes the present situation so excruciating is that if the price of Brent Crude really does drift down from $115 a barrel to $50 or $60 it would be incredibly bullish. As for the U.S., if a Grand Bargain miraculously appeared or if the economic recovery becomes self-reinforcing, U.S. equities could rally 20% fast. I wouldn't want to miss it! On the other hand, another financial crisis could take the S&P 500 down 20%. How do you invest your clients' and your family's money in such a circumstance?

■ ■ ■

May 29, 2012

*D*espite spending enormous amounts of time and money researching China and the price of oil, I believe the truth is "nobody knows nuthin' about either. Both are intricately complex, torturously convoluted, and very opaque. "Riddles wrapped in an enigma inside a mystery," as Churchill once described Russia. In the arena of horse manure dissemination, this creates a fertile environment for self-proclaimed experts and wise men to pontificate loudly and with great conviction while citing mysterious, inside sources and arcane theories. Every few months with much fanfare new books about oil and China are published, and the authors are dutifully interviewed by Charlie Rose leading to a new law: *The more books and scholarly treatises published on a subject, the less value there is in the books.* In other words, avoid them. The world record holder and leader in babble is investment books, to which this writer admits to have been a contributing polluter.

Now, shamelessly, I proceed to write a murky piece about the price of oil premised on transcendental information. What follows is a reflection of a conversation I just had with an elderly, elegant, aristocratic Saudi. The man is very rich and presumably well connected (but you never know), but he is not part of the extended Saudi royal family. He is not ostentatious or a name-dropper. In many ways he is the Davos man— Savile Row suit, Hermes tie, erudite, philosophical. He did not initiate the conversation. In the course of a lunch I asked him about the outlook for Saudi Arabia over the next several years. He was pessimistic citing the inflation and the underemployment of the young.

Proven Oil Reserves 2010 in Billions of Barrels

Saudi Arabia	262.4
Canada	175.2
Iran	137.6
Iraq	115.0
Kuwait	104.0
Venezuela	99.4
United Arab Emirates	97.8
Russia	60.0
Libya	44.3
Nigeria	37.2

Source: Energy Information Administration, Department of Energy

"But you are still rich and have the oil," I said.

"True, but you have to understand our geopolitical equation and vulnerability," he said calmly but intensely. "Our two most dangerous enemies are Iraq and Iran. Both are Shi'a and both are trying to destabilize the Arab world and our Sunni kingdom by funding terrorism. Our only weapons against them are our wealth and our oil. Their current vulnerability is their financial fragility. Their financial reserves are a fraction of ours and they desperately need money to prop up their economies. The ruling council has decided that over the next two years we have a brief window of opportunity to impoverish and weaken them by driving down the price of oil. Iraq and Iran need to produce and sell their oil at well over one hundred dollars a barrel. In the next 24 months we will gradually increase our production with the objective of breaking the price of crude down to $60 a barrel. Aramco is raising its capacity to produce significantly more crude. Note that at the same time Iraq, Russia, and Libya are already increasing their exports, and Iran and Venezuela also need to sell more. Strategic reserves in the consuming countries all over the world have been topped out, and large amounts of oil are stored in tankers."

"But these strategic reserves and floating inventories are relatively small amounts," I argued.

"True, but it's supply at the margin, and don't forget we have the wind at our backs because of Europe's problems and the weak global economy. Under *normal* recessionary circumstances we would be reducing production to maintain current prices. Instead we will be flooding a weak market already suffering indigestion. You also should understand that Kuwait and the United Arab Emirates are with us. Royal families tend to stick together."

"What about OPEC?" I asked. "Won't they reduce their production to maintain the price at over a hundred dollars a barrel?"

He laughed. "In extremis OPEC and the others always cheat and produce beyond their quotas. They are self-indulgent adolescents who count on us to be the balance wheel." He went on to point out that a new negative factor in the oil equation is natural gas whose supply is burgeoning because of fracking. "Natural gas has never been so cheap in relation to crude," he said. "In 10 years with the age of austerity in America and Europe hybrid and electric vehicles will be everywhere powered by electricity from natural gas. As for China, they will suffocate in their own pollution if they don't go electric."

He gestured with his soft, exquisitely manicured hands. "Sometimes I wonder if we will be able as planned to stabilize the price of crude so

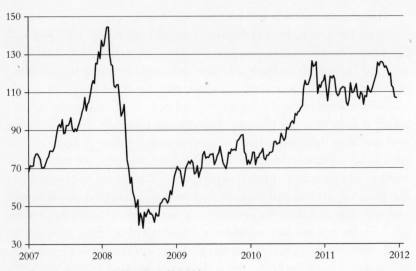

Ice Brent Futures 6/8/07–5/25/12

smoothly at around 60. Now there is an Iran-Hormuz risk premium in the quotation of perhaps $20. Maybe eventually there will be a psychospeculative, electric car discount. Perhaps as the price erodes month after month and the U.S. becomes self-sufficient in energy, the commodity speculators will move to another game and selling will beget selling. We could lose control and the price could fall to $40 or $50 a barrel. Price wars always get worse than you think. Don't forget Brent futures traded between 40 and 60 for six months less than four years ago."

"Won't all this be very painful for the kingdom?" I asked. "You have large youth unemployment and a rapidly growing idle and potentially restless population. We read your budget goes into deficit at eighty dollars a barrel. How can you afford this strategy?"

"The breakeven is more like 60 to 70," he told me. "We have huge oil and financial reserves. Yes, we will have to endure deficits and live off our own fat for a few years. The members of the extended royal family will bear most of the burden, but they seem to understand that it must happen. They realize the natives are sullen but not yet mutinous. We can afford the reduction in our income for a while. Iraq and Iran can't and will be strapped and much less inclined to fund revolutions and suicide bombers."

My conclusion: Do I believe this guy? Maybe. His story is plausible. Certainly I want to believe because it's very bullish although it wreaks long-term havoc with my energy-related holdings. I think he believes it. He is actually quite negative on Saudi Arabia. He thinks a lot of investment money will come out of the country.

What could go wrong? Israel could attack Iran. The Saudi royal family could change its mind. The rest of OPEC could reduce production. The Iranians could shut the Straits of Hormuz. The terrorists could mount a really serious effort to blow up the Saudi lifting facilities and disrupt production.

However, if it happens and Saudi Arabia succeeds in dramatically reducing the price of oil, it will be a transforming event. I think it's fundamentally very positive for the world economy, the oil-importing and -consuming countries, and world stock markets. A major reduction in the price of oil would be like a giant tax cut, which is just what this sickly old world needs. It's not bullish for the oil exporting countries, for their politicians and dictators, for commodity prices, the oil companies, the oil service sector and everything related to it. It's also disinflationary. I'm not sure what it does to other industrial commodity prices, alternative energy sources, and the fracking boom. Inevitably some large, fat bodies will come to the surface belly up.

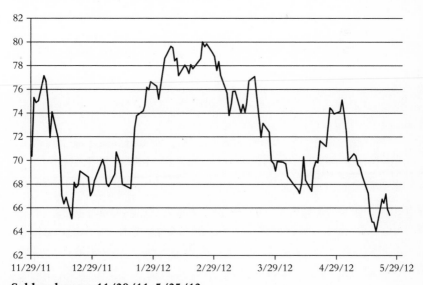

Schlumberger 11/29/11–5/25/12

Also carefully bear in mind that my man is talking about two years not two months. If for whatever reason the global economy (the U.S., China, and Europe) starts to do better, the price of oil will have a big rally. Presently oil and the energy stocks are a risk-on trade. I have learned that being early is the same as being wrong. I conclude that nevertheless his story is something to bear in mind. Take a look at the ugly chart of the once beautiful Schlumberger.

Meanwhile the Saudis perfectly reasonably are hedging their bets. Last week they signed a $3 billion contract with British Aerospace to provide for the training jets and combat management of the new fighter jets the Saudi Royal Air Force has purchased. The best, high-performance jets don't protect you from suicide bombers, but obviously they could be handy in preventing the bad guys' aircraft from blitzing your oil lifting installations or in a shooting war in the Gulf.

Conclusion

*A*s I reflect on this crisis period so stuffed with opportunity but also so full of pain and terror, I am struck with how hard it is to be an investor and a fiduciary. When managing risk in a portfolio, as a fiduciary of other people's money and also of your own and your family's, you always have to remember that there is the possibility of a catastrophic outcome. Jack Bogle, a veteran of many battles, said in a speech in 2009: "We must base our asset allocation not on the probabilities of choosing the right allocation but on the consequences of choosing the wrong allocation." He is completely and absolutely right!

On many grim afternoons in the long hot summer of 2011, as stocks plummeted as if presaging the end of the world, that thought tortured me. The history of the world is one of progress, and as a congenital optimist, I believe in equities. Fundamentally, in the long run you want to be an owner, not a lender. However, you always have to bear in mind that this time truly may be different, as Reinhart and Rogoff so eloquently preach. Remember the 1930s, Japan in the late 1990s, and then, of course, as Rogoff said once with a sly smile, there is that period of human history known as "the Dark Ages and it lasted 300 years."

As investors, we also always have to be aware of our innate and very human tendency to be fighting the last war. We forget that Mr. Market is an ingenious sadist, and that he delights in torturing us in different ways. In 2008, I was not respectful enough of the message of the markets and of my ignorance in not understanding the depths of the housing mortgage cancer. After a very strong run in the previous five years, I suffered a big drawdown in that year. The fact that I was off significantly less than the S&P 500, MSCI World, and the MSCI Emerging Markets Indices, which were off 37%, 41%, and 53%, respectively, was of scant and cold consolation to my investors.

A 40% gain in 2009 and a good number in 2010 only got me back to my high water mark of 2007. Clients didn't like the big loss year and the volatility. Neither did my partners. Neither did I, for that matter. There were redemptions. Fundamentally, I do not believe in stop loss orders for individual positions or for portfolios. If the valuations have shrunk, and if you are convinced the fundamentals of your investment thesis are still intact, why should you be bullied by temporarily falling prices? Mr. Market is a manic depressive with huge mood swings, and you should bet against him, not with him, particularly when he is raving.

Of course, the answer to that question is that perhaps there is something happening out there that you just plain don't understand. But Buffett, a man like me who believes in America and the Tooth Fairy, presents the dilemma best. It's as though you are in business with a partner who has a bipolar personality. When your partner is deeply distressed, depressed, and in a dark mood and offers to sell his share of the business at a huge discount, you should buy it. When he is ebullient and optimistic and wants to buy your share from you at an exorbitant premium, you should oblige him. As usual, Buffett makes it sound easier than it is because measuring the level of intensity of the mood swings of your bipolar partner is far from an exact science.

In any case, in 2010, I committed to my partners and investors that I would never again to the best of my abilities allow myself to lose significantly more than 10% from the opening value of my fund at the beginning of the year. I consoled myself that many of the allegedly great macro proprietary traders practice a similar discipline with both themselves and their minions except that they enforce it as a 10% drawdown from a high water mark at any time in the course of a year. A 10% loss limit means that when you get down to around 8% you have to begin taking off risk dramatically because one bad day can bang you through. The truth of the matter is that the bottom is always, without fail, 10% below your worst-case expectation.

After modest gains in the first half of the year, in the long, hot summer of 2011, the S&P 500 plummeted 17% from July 22 to August 8, then rallied 10% in five trading days only to fall again to the lows, surge back even faster, and undercut the previous lows by the first trading day of October. Then, a powerful rally began that took the S&P 500 up to recover two-thirds of its summer loss, whereupon it stalled for the rest of what was a turbulent year. All summer I remained convinced we were in a rolling panic aided and abetted by the mindless madness of the momentum traders. Nevertheless, four times in seven weeks in July and August, with the sword of Damocles hanging over my head and bearing in mind the possibility of a "catastrophic outcome," I reduced my net long very substantially to make sure I didn't breach the sacred 10% loss commitment guideline.

The consequence was that I got brutally whipsawed. Even though I wrote an essay to my investors on the bottom day, October 3, 2011, saying it was time to begin loading up, I made only 7.5% in the month of October when the S&P 500 surged 11% and finished with a single-digit loss for the year. I had been brutally whipsawed or you might say, hoisted on my own petard. Trends can reverse for no apparent reason with incredible celerity. Fifty some years ago, Sir Alec Cairncross doodled it best:

A trend is a trend is a trend
But the question is, will it bend?
Will it alter its course
Through some unforeseen force
And come to a premature end?

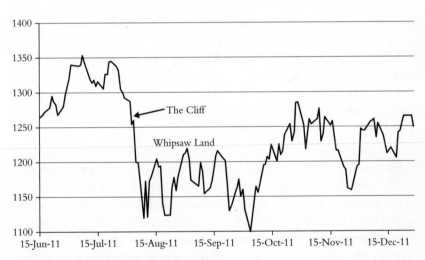

Summer of 2011 Panic and Volatility

Nations, institutions, and individuals always have had and still have a powerful tendency to prepare themselves to fight the last war. During and after a prolonged and devastating secular bear market such as we are currently experiencing, investors naturally abhor volatility and search for vehicles that will provide stable returns. They will gladly sacrifice higher returns for lower volatility. For the true investor with a long-term horizon, this doesn't make sense. Buffett put it best when he said he would always pick an investment strategy that over five years could give him a 12% compounded annual return, but that was volatile over one that promised a stable 8% return annually. Today, big pools of money around the world are allocating to the stable 8%s. I think they're wrong. This obviously is a self-serving comment on my part since I'm volatile.

But what's the moral of this story? Know thyself and know thy foibles. Study the history of your emotions and your actions. At the extreme moments of fear and greed, the power of the daily price momentum and the mood and passions of "the crowd" are tremendously important psychological influences on you. It takes a strong, self-confident, emotionally mature person to stand firm against disdain, mockery, and repudiation when the market itself seems to be absolutely confirming that you are both mad and wrong. Also, be obsessive in making sure your facts are right and that you haven't missed or misunderstood something.

Beware of committing to mechanistic investing rules such as stop-loss limits or other formulas. None of the old rules work anymore, but then they never did. Work very hard to better understand how you as an investor react to both prosperity and adversity, and particularly to the market's manic swings, both euphoric and traumatic. Keep an investment diary and re-read it from time to time but particularly at moments when there is tremendous exuberance and also panic. We are in a very emotional business, and any wisdom we can extract from our own experience is very valuable. And waste time only with people you like.

For instance, I know I had a tendency at both extremes to be early. I got bullish two months too soon in January 2009 and lost 9%, but in 1999, I got very bearish on technology and the Internet stocks and sold them heavily in December. The NASDAQ index peaked on March 10 at 5048 and bottomed on October 4, 2002, at 1139. Brilliant? Hardly. In 1999, the index itself rose in three months 35% to 40% from the levels where I was selling in 1999 to its March 10 high and many hot, Internet stocks doubled. Some very important clients, when they received my year-end reviews of their portfolios, were appalled at my drastically reduced holding of technology and with recriminations and gusto closed their accounts. By some I was gently told they were sorry but it was a new world and they wanted to move on. By others I was rudely informed that I was senile and the world had passed me by. You'll never know who your friends are until you've had a bad year.

Understanding the effect of emotion on your actions has never been more important than it is now. In the midst of this great financial and economic crisis that grips the world, central banks are printing money in one form or another. This makes our investment world even more prone to bubbles and panics than it has been in the past. Either plague can kill you.

This diary begins in the summer of 2010. Diaries, if they are to be meaningful, have to be immersed in the full context of the total state of mind of the writer because actions and reactions, of course, are deeply affected by the mood swings of the diarist. A motley multitude of frivolous diaries litter the landscape, but I have read and found great sustenance in diaries focused on Berlin in the late 1930s, and the perceptive and sensitive combat diaries of Guadalcanal, the Korean War, Dien Ben Phu, and Vietnam. Investment life also is combat.

The stresses of life are not just mental. The physical condition of the participant intrudes as well. In *Sea of Thunder* (Simon & Schuster, 2006), the author Evan Thomas describes how on the American warships late in the Pacific war the long stretches of physical inactivity at sea and the lack of exercise wore on the officers, causing restlessness, insomnia, constipation, and debilitating nervous afflictions. These ailments often resulted in erratic decision making and behavior. Insomnia in particularly is the pernicious disease of the stressed investment manager, and it can be a very serious affliction. In the summer of 2011, for a variety of reasons, I was not sleeping well. Two in the morning is not the time for investment introspection. You don't make good decisions in the middle of the night or when you're exhausted. I always try to keep exercising and to have an inventory of Ambien handy.

Thus I inject herein detail on my state of mind over the time period covered. By the summer of 2010, unbeknownst to me, my left hip was deteriorating. Hiking, mountain climbing, and singles tennis are very important parts of my life. For years I have played singles tennis every weekend and holiday with friends, many of whom are investors. Invariably afterwards a group of us would have extended, candid, intimate investment chats. As I describe this interaction, perhaps it sounds ridiculous but it was a perfect combination of highly competitive physical activity, which temporarily purged your mind of market-related afflictions, followed by investment stimulation. The participants ranged from other hedge fund and long-only guys to the best economist in the world and the manager of a major endowment. In the winter we played indoors at 7:30 in the morning and had coffee at nine.

As my hip tightened and became painful, my ability to move quickly deteriorated and I began to consistently lose in the tennis. It sounds ridiculous, but I cared and it was depressing. Also in the summer of 2010, as part of a group of friends, I took my teenage grandchildren to climb in both China and Japan. I had fairly easily climbed Mt. Fuji twice before, but this time on the second day of the climb I ran out of gas a thousand feet from the summit. It was not an uplifting experience. Was it the hip or my motor that was failing? I didn't know.

In any case by the spring of 2011 it was clear that stretching and physical therapy was not going to be the answer, and I became reconciled to having an operation. I had literally not had an operation or spent a night in a hospital for over 40 years. Also my hip was giving me considerable pain, and the prescribed painkillers made me feel lousy. When I had the operation on July 11 it was successful, but the aftereffects on my body were about as bad as I expected. The time at an acute rehab facility from July 14 to July 21 was a glimpse into the waiting room for hell. I describe this experience in more detail in my December 14, 2011 piece "Another Tsunami" earlier in the book. The rehab was boring, tedious, uncomfortable, and grim. The food was inedible. In summary, during that summer of my discontent the aftereffects and consequences of the hip procedure merged with the volatility, violence, and wealth destruction of the equity markets to sap my ebullience.

However, Mr. Market and clients don't give a hoot about your hip or mental state. You still have to perform and make the right decisions. My point is that you have to recognize what is happening to you and your ability to make good decisions. Obviously family is indispensable, but my other solutions are exercise, talking to other investors who are friends and who also are suffering, working, Ambien to make sure you sleep, and also luxuriating with a glass of good chardonnay and reading a powerful, well-written novel or history. The summer of 2011 I got a lot of solace from reading about the later life of Theodore Roosevelt and the story of Catherine the Great.

Every investor is different and everyone has his or her own releases. Family, gardening, charitable activities, church—whatever works for you. Figure it out, and when the stress mounts, stick to your routines. They are even more important when you are doing badly than when you are prospering, although hubris is a deadly disease. Above all, don't desert your releases because you are doing badly. They are important in good times as in bad in maintaining the emotional equilibrium that is so essential for good decision making. Spending more time at the office and not going to the gym or whatever so you can listen to one more conference call is the wrong time allocation.

Repeat endlessly: "This too shall pass."